ADULTERY FOR ADULTS

ADULTERY FOR ADULTS

An Unique Guide to
Self-Development

by

Joyce Peterson and Marilyn Mercer

COWARD-McCANN, INC.

NEW YORK

Second Impression

Copyright © 1968
by Joyce Peterson and Marilyn Mercer

Library of Congress Catalog
Card Number: 68–8574

PRINTED IN THE UNITED STATES OF AMERICA

DEDICATION

To Alice, Bill, Charlie, Don, Evelyn, Frank, Gladys,
Henry, Irene, John, Kathleen, Lenny, Muriel, Norman,
Olga, Pete, Queenie, Robert, Sally, Teddy, Ursula,
Vincent, Wendy, Xavier, Yvonne, Zachary,
Dr. Masters, Mrs. Johnson, and Eddie.

Contents

7

Preface

It is widely accepted in society today that sexual adventure is the province of the young. Those teen-agers with their pot and promiscuity; those Ivy League undergraduates holding press conferences to discuss their irregular living arrangements—it would seem that the under-30 generation has all the fun. However, if you follow accounts of their carryings on about anomie, or alienation, or whatever it is they are complaining about, you will soon realize that they don't have any fun *at all*. Else why would they need all that LSD? "If youth but knew; if age but could." But that's just the point. It *can*.

Introduction

We would like to make it clear at the beginning that we are not, God forbid, opposed to marriage and the family. Quite the contrary. We maintain that creative adultery, practiced according to the rules in this book, is a constructive alternative to multiple divorce and remarriage, with the consequent multiple alimony payments and confused children. That adultery tends, in fact, to preserve the institution of marriage—along, of course, with its other fringe benefits.

We have given rules for married men and married women who wish to involve themselves in extramarital liaisons—more rules, it turns out, for women, but only because they seem to need guidance more. (There is also a helpful chapter for single people.) Parallel his and hers hints are given in many instances, though not in all— sometimes because parallel situations don't exist, sometimes because the whole thing gets too complicated. Consequently, we speak sometimes to the woman, sometimes to the man, according to no set plan and with a certain charming insouciance or perhaps lack of organization.

Don't try to sort it out; just read everything. Most of the advice is cross-applicable.

ADULTERY FOR ADULTS

CHAPTER ONE

The Case for Creative Adultery

DULTERY IS AMERICA'S MOST POPU-
LAR SPORT, BUT IT IS THE ONLY
SPORT FOR WHICH OFFICIAL RULES
do not exist. This book fills that need.

If you look around you, you will see that most people
who play this game come out losers. That's because they
don't know the rules. (They are, so to speak, playing in
the dark.) There is nothing wrong with the game. Only
with the players. They mess up.

There are, of course, some popular ideas that people
think are rules being bandied about. You get them from
all sorts of unreliable sources. Psychiatrists. Magazines.
Your mother. These are not, repeat not, the real rules, and
if you follow them, you are bound to come out a loser.
(The people who make these rules want it that way—you
didn't know that, did you?)

Rules such as:

Adultery is wrong. (David Susskind)

Adultery is an early warning symptom of the male
menopause. (*Ladies' Home Journal, McCall's*, etc.)

Adultery is neat, but only if you can make the man
marry you, and he probably won't, so be prepared to
be miserable. (*Cosmopolitan*)

Adultery is probably all right for fellows who are old
enough to get married. (*Playboy*)

Adultery is OK if it is a meaningful relationship, but
wouldn't it be better to explore more fully the mean-
ing of the meaningful relationship you are already
lousing up? (Psychiatrist)

If you have to get mixed up with somebody, why
couldn't it be Jackie Kennedy/Nelson Rockefeller?
(Your mother)

Remember, when taking advice from a marriage coun-
selor, your sister-in-law, or your psychiatric social worker
—those who can't, teach.

The Theory of Horizontal Enrichment

The real trouble with the above rules is that they were
invented for (sometimes by) children, and adultery is, of
course, for adults. A still-young couple may well find
themselves with all the things they have been working for
accomplished. The children are grown or at least de-
parted for the East Village. The washing machine is paid
for. There are two cars in the garage. Life no longer
presents a challenge. They may well look at each other in
dismay and ask: Is that all? Well, it isn't. This is the time
of life to cast your eyes about you and seek out new and
challenging relationships to broaden your horizons and
add new dimensions to your already very comfortable life.
This is called horizontal enrichment.

Of course, the theory can be practiced successfully by
the very young, too, but usually only if: (1) they are
exceptionally intelligent; (2) they are exceptionally rich;
or (3) it is, in fact, Jackie Kennedy/Nelson Rockefeller.

It is especially important for women to understand this theory. We all are familiar with the housewife's complaint: what to do when the children are grown. Many solutions occur—marketing your peach chutney, taking an MA in psychiatric social work, drinking. But these are either self-destructive or too hard. The mature years are not for going back to school all over again or taking some dopey job you wouldn't be any good at anyway. They are for creative living.

An intimate relationship with another person brings the totality of another consciousness into your orbit for a mutually enriching experience. It broadens your horizons, increases your understanding of your fellowman and your knowledge of the world. It makes you better able to relate to others. It makes you in every way a better person.

Why, then, confine yourself for a lifetime to one such relationship when you could have lots? That's pretty silly, isn't it?

Moreover, besides improving you as an individual, it strengthens marriage. There's a lot of feedback from all that self-improvement. Your new outside relationships keep you and your spouse alert and alive, open vistas that you can share. They relieve the tensions that can result from overdependence. All of this, of course, is highly beneficial to the family unit: Happy parents make happy children.

Adultery: A Civil Right of Women . . .

Women have earned the right to vote, to work, to smoke cigarettes, and, thanks largely to the efforts on their behalf by our colleague Mrs. Helen Gurley Brown, to indulge in premarital relationships without censure. Sex and the single girl is all very well—but what about sex and the married girl? This is the last frontier.

And Men, Too

Although men traditionally, under the double standard that obtains, are less subject to criticism if they seek relationships outside marriage, in recent years they have, in public opinion, been sent back to the kitchen. During the recent togetherness era, the role of the male in our society was construed as not only breadwinner, but homemaker, handyman, and baby-sitter as well. Father, after a hard day at the office, was supposed to come home and wash dishes, change diapers, and mop floors. Mother was supposed to run around in pants, fixing washing machines and plastering walls. Or, as an alternative, she was urged to realize her full potential by going out and getting a job as a vice-president of General Motors. The roles of the sexes become totally confused. Betty Friedan told women they should be men; Ashley Montagu told men they should be women.

This is not the way things are supposed to be *at all*. In fact, that way lies unisex. (Marshall McLuhan thinks this is a good idea, but he's wrong.) Men are not supposed to run vacuum cleaners or spend all day Saturday playing baseball with children. They are supposed to come home in the evening, demand their pipe and slippers, and roar at the children if they are interrupted while reading the evening paper. Moreover, they are supposed to spend their leisure-time weekends deep-sea fishing, getting involved in all-night poker games, drinking, or engaging in other masculine pursuits. Women, on the other hand, are not supposed to fix the plumbing or be presidents of companies. They are supposed to lollygag around all day reading *Vogue* and painting their fingernails, emerging in the evening only to kiss the children, let them admire their lovely mother for a moment, and then off to the ball. But nobody dares. Everybody has been brainwashed.

How to reverse this situation and bring things right again? In many cases, it may be too late. Some couples are hopelessly mired in this concept and can find no remedy within the marriage. However, a romantic attachment outside marriage—a new lady friend who thinks the poor downtrodden husband is a tiger; a gentleman who thinks the wife is a cross between Jacqueline Kennedy and Julie Christie can do much to restore the proper self-images of both partners. In short, adultery can restore man's masculinity and women's feminity—and about time, too—and human dignity on both sides.

Some First Principles

In order to achieve the ideal adulterous relationship, it is necessary to go back to some first principles about the relationship of the sexes in general. A great deal has been written on this subject; consequently, misconceptions abound. One of the biggest misconceptions is summed up in the phrase "the war between men and women."

Since prehistory, men and women have been persuaded in various ways that their relationship is a competitive one. Someone must win. *Ergo,* someone must lose. This is wrong.

Consider the popular phrases "to catch a man"; to "trap

him." And on the man's side, "to make out"; "to score." They presuppose a situation in which women are out to obtain support, social position, money, adulation, deference, love, Hondas, sable coats, trips to St. Moritz, whatever it is they're after, from some poor, defenseless male, offering in exchange as little as they can get away with. Men, on the other hand, are out to obtain a maximum of sex with a minimum of commitment. This leads to a contest and ultimately to mutual hostility and suspicion of motives, which can mar, sometimes beyond repair, the possibility of the nicest relationship life has to offer.

Many miserable marriages are built on these attitudes. A man who thinks this way may marry as a compromise, reasoning that the stability of marriage will provide him with clean shirts, regular meals, and, as G. B. Shaw used to say, "the maximum of temptation with the maximum of opportunity." The woman may marry in a flat panic at twenty-five, thinking it is now or never. Fred may not be the best thing on her horizon, but he asked her, and that's enough. (Unlike that rotten radical writer who sampled and ran.)

Young sex, the struggle to survive, small children—the delights of the nest—will sustain them for fifteen years, but then, watch out. At this point, battles that once were resolved with kisses and tears tend to result in a steady widening of the breach that was there, though unnoticed, from the beginning. They both feel that they've been had, and indeed they have.

She is envious of what she considers his involvement with the real, gay, exciting world outside and at the office. She feels the pangs of boredom, tedium and drudgery as he runs happily off to the train. She has a tiresome day, greets him with sulks and a martini on her breath instead of on a tray, and so the battle lines are drawn.

People are likely to conclude from observing this tiresome and dreary pattern that men and women are basically incompatible—that the best that can be hoped for is a prolonged cease-fire in a cold war.

An adulterous relationship, if started for the wrong reasons, can founder on the same rocks. It is less likely to happen in an adulterous relationship, however: Nothing tends to make people behave in a civilized fashion more than the knowledge that both can walk out at any time. In fact, one of the joys of adultery is the realization that there is nothing in the relationship but the relationship itself. However, competitiveness between the sexes destroys a liaison as quickly as—or more quickly than—a marriage.

WORDS TO LIVE BY

"Make love, not war."

The Ideal Adulterous Relationship

Don't shoot crap with gamblers, don't play cards with strangers, and don't go to bed with anybody whose troubles are worse than your own.

—NELSON ALGREN

The ideal adulterous relationship is more often achieved by those who are already happily married. As partners they have been thoroughly tested; they bear, so to speak, the *Good Housekeeping* Seal of Approval. If you are contemplating a liaison with somebody who is un-married, be sure that he or she is *very happily* unmar-ried—and even then, proceed with caution. (Although some of the most successful relationships have come out of that imbalance—but more of that later.) The ideal adulterous relationship must proceed according to strict rules. The first and most basic: *Never* think in terms of marriage. You are already married, remember? Divorce and remarriage are not the point at all. The point of horizontal enrichment is to enjoy simultaneously a new and absorbing relationship and the comfort and security of your old marriage. There must be something holding your old marriage together. Your retirement investment plan? Color television? Whatever it is, don't lose it. Build on what you have. Second cardinal rule: No complaining, no explaining. Do not make excessive emotional demands on your partner or whine and complain over fancied slights. Adultery is supposed to be a *fun* relationship. Make appointments ahead of time, and observe them. If you must break them, do so in advance. Play fair. Indeed the rules for successful adultery are the same as those for any kind of civilized social intercourse. How simple to observe them. And yet there are many who don't.

Sixteen Reasons Why Adultery Is Good for You

It makes you a better person.
It strengthens your marriage.
It makes your children more secure.
It is good for your general health.
It makes a psychiatrist unnecessary.
You watch your weight.

You exercise.

It is nonfattening.

It does not rot your teeth.

It improves your grooming.

It improves your posture.

It improves your eyesight.

It makes men more masculine, women more feminine.

It curbs juvenile delinquency.

It helps the national economy.

It can, on occasion, be tax deductible.*

Adultery eliminates the need for divorce, stabilizes the family and, ultimately, society as a whole. Carrying this thinking to its logical conclusion could put an end to war, poverty, the crisis in our cities, and conceivably air pollution.

* To the Collector of Internal Revenue: Our lawyer, who has a very literal mind, told us to take this out. However, we feel that it is a needed, tacit comment on the sorry state of contemporary morality, as regards tax matters. Double check those expense accounts!

CHAPTER TWO

A Few Historical Notes

DULTERY HAS HAD ITS UPS AND DOWNS THROUGHOUT HISTORY. IT HAS BEEN PUNISHABLE BY DEATH, tossing in the river, beheading, stoning, public censure, and chopping off various parts of the anatomy—noses, fingers, and such—but somehow it has never quite lost its attraction.

The Ancient World

In ancient Egypt it was considered too good for the fellahin—they couldn't commit adultery for the simple reason that they couldn't marry. They could carry on like the beasts in the field if they wished, but marriages by contract, with the resultant joys of *breaking* the contract, were for the aristocracy.

The Babylonians, despite the bad name they have in the Bible, took a very hard-nosed attitude toward female adultery. Adulteresses risked being tied up, so they couldn't even dog-paddle, and thrown in the river. If a wife and her lover were found sinning, they both were trussed up, and plosh, into the river. If they were merely suspect, into the river again, but untied, so they could prove their innocence by swimming. If they couldn't swim, well . . . *tant pis.*

The ancient Arabs had some harsh punishments for adultery—death, for example—but Mohammed, who married a pretty girl when he was getting on a bit, reduced this to flogging. And a good thing, too, since his wife, Ayesha, was subsequently accused of dillydallying with a soldier. The Prophet, known for his wisdom, also made a law saying that anyone who accused anyone else of adultery had to bring along *four* witnesses to prove it, and if they couldn't, well, eighty lashes to them. This put an end to all sorts of bad mouthing.

Classical Antiquity

Plato, never a lady's man, advocated passing a law that married men should be forbidden to have anything to do with any women but their own wives. No hetaerae, no slave girls, no nothing. This naturally went over like a lead balloon with the ancient Greeks who preferred almost *anything* to their own wives. In *The Republic,* Plato then advocated free love for everybody, but this never came about because it seemed a bit extreme. In his old age Plato finally found the ideal Greek way, acceptable to everybody. He said that married people should be permitted to run around, provided they were discreet about it, and *scandal avoided*.

The Romans were never picky about virginity or marital fidelity. They felt, in fact, that nothing created a relationship more binding than sex. Friendship and comradeship were all right, but Roman citizens liked a more lasting arrangement. In fact, they used sex to seal a bargain in the same way that we today might have something notarized. Nothing if not practical, a Roman committed adultery for all sorts of secondary reasons—for example, with his mother-in-law so he could become emperor, things like that—but these are essentially business relationships and not the concern of this book.

The Age of Chivalry

Adultery had its finest hour in the Middle Ages when it was the number one pastime of the upper classes. The lower classes had to work too hard and didn't wash enough, so it was *out* for them, but their betters more than made up for what they missed. Every knight had to have his lady to be devoted to, so he could joust for her and carry her scarf and all. If a knight were given a hard time, he would apply straight to the Virgin Mary for help. Asking the Virgin Mary for help in seducing the local seigneur's wife might be compared today to writing to the Vatican for help in seducing your Aunt Lottie, but in the Middle Ages, people seemed to think it was all right. The church didn't really mind what people did so long as they tithed.

There's a lot of talk about how all the romantics did in those days was to play their lutes and moon and write poetry, but that's not true at all. There was a lot of climbing of towers and sneaking through stone passageways and hiding in cupboards and things like that. They had a grand time.

The middle classes who were observing all this seemed to think that nothing was going on because nobody actually came right out and *said* so. And when the knight-errant *was* accused, he just said *honi soit qui mal y pense* to YOU, and that shut them up, you can be sure.

Marriage was considered a good way to get ahead in the world, and necessary to legitimize children, but it had very little to do with romance. Everyone knows about Isolde, but can anyone tell you the name of Tristan's wife? You didn't know he *had* a wife. Well, *Isolde* knew, but she didn't care, because in the Middle Ages "love" was the big status word (it might be compared with "creativity" today, to give you the idea), and if you *loved* somebody, anything you did was OK, provided you didn't get caught.

By the end of the fourteenth century the system had begun to break down because the middle classes had begun to imitate. The burghers had to do what the aristocracy was doing. Of course, serious, sedate, and upward mobile, they took the minnesingers at their word (it's as if you believed a rock-and-roll singer who says he will *die* of love), so there was a lot of sighing and scarf carrying and nothing else.

You *know* it, the whole thing went out of style in a hurry. (To give you just one more insight into the burgher mentality—they invented the chastity belt.)

Well, as we said, the burghers killed off the Age of Chivalry, and a hundred years went by, and then the Thirty Years War almost killed off everybody, before it all started to sort out again and the simpler joys of life were restored.

The Age of Gallantry

In the seventeenth century the Age of Gallantry dawned, and it became so obligatory for fashionable people to have lovers and mistresses that many people married just to have someone to be unfaithful to. In eighteenth-century France anyone who didn't run around was looked upon with suspicion. Sort of like an American businessman who refuses to play golf. We mean, it would just make you *wonder* about that person.

When the English, nastily, beheaded Charles I, and the French did likewise to Louis XVI, people suddenly became very sober and serious, and they have remained so right down to modern times. Queen Victoria had a perfectly terrible effect on people and made everyone very perverse and morose and inclined to beat their children, and people are just finally getting over *that*. So adultery is in an ambiguous state today.

The Modern World

In America, at least until recently, it has been in low repute, primarily because of the actual and ever-present possibility of divorce and remarriage. (And the image hasn't been helped any, either, by spoilsports like John Updike.) However, in the Latin countries, France and Italy notably, the fact that divorce is unobtainable has given adultery the dignified status it requires. In Italy the game has gained considerable additional cachet because once in a while someone gets killed, elevating the game in the minds of many critics to an art form on a level with bullfighting.

It's unlikely that in our contemporary computerized society, in which the sexes more and more tend to dress alike, look alike and act alike, and with its young people whose idea of pleasure is turning on with banana peels and whose idea of love is handing somebody a flower, for heaven's sake, that we will ever totally recapture the glories of the past. It is, let's face it, an uphill fight. But let us at least take these long-dead heroes as examples and try.

CHAPTER THREE

How to Begin

AUNCHING YOURSELF ON A CAREER OF CREATIVE ADULTERY IS NOT EASY. TO BEGIN WITH, IF YOU HAVE established a reputation as a pillar of your community, nobody is going to believe you when you start out in search of your new life, and so you will have difficulty in finding partners. The first step, then, is to change your image. As the processes are different for the two sexes, we will consider them separately.

Procedures for Women

Let's assume you are a middle-class American housewife with twenty years of service in child rearing, PTA attending, den mothering, or whatever it is that middle-class housewives are supposed to do, with only a few lapses into fits of the sulks upon rereading *The Feminine Mystique.* You may well have smooched in the kitchen with your best friend's husband once or twice or cast a shy glance at the lifeguard at the country club pool, but never have you followed through. Now you are about to. Scary, isn't it?

First, some things not to do.

The obvious. You can't suddenly start getting yourself up like an early Rita Hayworth pinup or jumping on top of pianos and singing torch songs. People will think you have flipped. A good example is Flora W., whose idea of announcing her availability was to appear suddenly in cleavage to the waist and do things like nibbling on men's earlobes while dancing, growling softly all the while. However, instead of launching herself on an adulterous career, as was her intention, she inadvertently launched her husband. A man with a loony wife is obvious and, indeed, fair game. So. Forewarned is forearmed. Don't go around acting like a nut.

Do not be the aggressor. At first, at least. (Although there are exceptions for advanced players.) However, for the purposes of this chapter, which is for neophytes, we will assume that man is the pursuer, woman the pursued.

Your Basic Problem

Your basic problem is that in your circle you are known as good old Walter's wife. Sad, but there it is. A point to bear in mind here (as well as throughout your career in romantic adventure) is that men are the idealists, women the realists.

The basic hang-up of the red-blooded, straight-arrow American male (and who would want any other kind?) is that he is helplessly torn between moral self-justification and the desire to be a swinger. (This attitude is generally traced to the Protestant ethic that is said to cripple our society in so many ways, but we have observed it all too often among Catholics, Jews, Unitarians, and indeed some members of the Neo-American Church.)

None of these sterling types can in good conscience

take up with good old Walter's wife, no matter how much he may secretly wish to. What to do? Become somebody else, of course.

A Bad Reputation, or, What's Bad About It?

What you have to do, basically, is establish a bad reputation. If you acquire a bad reputation, it doesn't matter whose good old wife you are; all bets are off.

First, change your appearance. If you have been going around in ill-fitting skirts and tennis shoes, start looking sleek and chic. If you have always gone about looking sleek and chic, switch to ill-fitting skirts and tennis shoes. (*Expensive* ill-fitting skirts; there is a difference between a country gentlewoman and a slob.) If your uniform up to now has been the little print dress and mink stole, try stark sheaths in blinding colors and big dark glasses. If you have been the outdoor girl with a year-round tan, develop an interesting pallor, grow your hair long, and wear funny-looking stockings. Consider getting yourself up like a British mod movie starlet at your discretion—remember the credibility gap.

It's a good idea, while making this changeover, to go off on a trip. When you come back looking different, everybody will assume that you have had an experience, even if all you did was visit your sister in Minneapolis.

The next step in establishing a bad reputation is changing your behavior pattern. Also, a reputation for erratic behavior ahead of time is a great help later on. When your behavior really becomes erratic, nobody will know the difference.

Changing Your Pattern: Some Things to Do

If you have been in the habit of chauffeuring the Little League on Tuesday afternoons or having lunch with the girls at the Pancake House on Thursdays, stop. Make some feeble excuse, such as you have decided to spend your afternoons learning to play the electric organ.

Start leaving your car in funny places, like overnight in front of the public library.

Make and receive mysterious phone calls. Arrange to have Western Union telephone you when you have friends in. Look horrified when you answer the phone, and explain loudly that you can't talk now. Western Union will think you are a little peculiar, but then, it's used to all kinds.

When your best friend drops by in the morning to borrow two dozen highball glasses and your chafing dish, ask her to wait outside for a few minutes. Then let her in, but don't let her out of the living room. Act nervous.

Buy $200 worth of new underwear, and show it to all your friends. Don't explain.

The Big Lie

If you sense that these techniques are not working for you, if you have tried them all conscientiously and people are still not talking about you—you will just have to do the talking yourself.

To start the ball rolling, make lunch dates with four or five of your most trustworthy women friends. Make the dates ahead of time, impressing upon each one that you have something important to discuss. Swear each one to secrecy, and then tell her that you desperately need her advice.

It seems you have been having an affair for the past four years with a big Wall Street type who will be nameless, but you are about to break it off because he is about to go into politics and his wife is threatening to divorce him, and furthermore his secretary saw you together at the corner of Lexington Avenue and Forty-ninth Street last Tuesday, and you are too frightened to go on. Should you go to Europe to get over it? Can she suggest a good psychiatrist (you don't really have to go), or should you just sit it out? Cry a little. While you're telling this story, make it as good as you can.

It adds verisimilitude, not to mention panache, actually to name the man, particularly if he is well known. Mistress (or ex-mistress) of a famous man is an intriguing image. If you don't know anybody famous, isn't there someone in your vicinity who carries the proper prestige? The president of the Town Council? The tennis pro? Lead guitar in your high school rock group?

Remember, you are never going to be asked for proof. One of the most successful careers in creative adultery we know of was launched by a young woman who simply went around telling everybody she was having an affair with John Kenneth Galbraith. After all, who do you know who is going to ask John Kenneth Galbraith?

Once you have satisfactorily established a bad reputation, it's time to close in for the kill. You are, of course, going to as many parties as you are asked to or can gracefully crash. You are going without your husband whenever possible. You are also involving yourself in whatever activities you feel may produce your particular Mr. Right —an extension course in Asian studies, protest marches, water-skiing—whatever best suits your style. Maximum exposure is the idea here. And, if you have followed the preceding rules carefully, admiring glances are being cast in your direction. You have only to return them—meaningfully—and you are on your way.

WORDS TO LIVE BY

"There are few good women who do not tire of their role."

—LA ROCHEFOUCAULD

Procedures for Men

Let us assume that you are a middle-class American male, exemplary husband and father, substantial income, standing in the community, lots of credit cards. You've always considered yourself, and have been considered by others, as a clean liver. Of course, there was that receptionist in the branch office in Cleveland. And there were those times at the Lumber and Plywood Management Association conferences in Puerto Rico—but trips don't count. And as you and your wife agreed the time she found out about the check-out girl at Bohack's, these passing infidelities are essentially meaningless—they don't affect your marriage in any real way. (Just don't let it happen again.)

Well, now you are about to do something that is essentially meaningful and can affect your marriage in lots of ways—if you do not think seriously and plan ahead.

Your aim is to embark on one, or a series of, long-term relationships in depth with charming and stimulating female companions, who share your adult approach to adultery. Who will conduct the affair from their end with grace and discretion. Who will not make waves. Serious ladies. Therefore, your approach to them, as opposed to, say, your approach to that meter maid who kept giving you parking tickets and waiting in your car to hand them to you, must be a serious one.

Approaches to Avoid

Don't, for example, start suddenly cutting up at parties, pinching women surreptitiously and making lewd remarks. This is sure death. (As far as party conversation goes, the rule is—Women: Talk about sex. Men: Never.)

To begin with, there are two interpretations of this kind of behavior, and neither does anything at all for your image. No one has a good word for Fletcher the Lecher in contemporary society. Most of the brighter women you know and all the ones who have psychiatrists will immediately assume that this behavior is a cover-up for—oh, all kinds of nameless and ominous inadequacies. What, they will ask suspiciously, is he trying to prove? You will not make points with them. The dumber ones will accept your behavior at face value and assume that you are indeed the great lover you present yourself as. But you will bomb out with them, too, since they will reason, with their tiny minds: Why join the crowd? There's no particular cachet in acquiring *you*. Perhaps they are not so dumb at that.

Just as the woman about to embark on a career of adultery, you, too, must change your image. If she has been known as good old Walter's wife, you, perhaps, have been known as good old Walter, and how boring can you get? We must change all that.

Changing Your Pattern: Some Things to Do

You must develop a new personality, but in a different fashion. You do not wish to establish a bad reputation— far from it. In fact, if you have one, it is wise at this point to start obliterating any traces. This is most easily done by undertaking some conspicuous good work. If you have been known up till now as something of a sport, teach a course in woodworking at the Y. Go to the Girl Scouts' father-daughter jamboree. You don't have to try too hard. Memories fade fast.

But we digress. Your real aim is to establish yourself as a fellow with hitherto unnoticed hidden depths. You must make every woman you know realize suddenly that there is more, much more, to old Walter than meets the eye. But this must be done with great subtlety. Each lady must think that she—and she alone—has discovered the real you, behind that thickening paunch and under that balding scalp.

FOR STARTERS, YOU MIGHT:

Buy a leather jacket.
Start wearing a cap—in town, a homburg.

Grow a mustache. (Not a beard; beards are ordinary.) A long, droopy one is best.

Develop a passionate interest in pre-Columbian art, rock-and-roll records, the writings of Teilhard de Chardin.

Buy a motorcycle (*not* a scooter), and roar around on it every Saturday.

Develop a secret sorrow. Go around looking thin-lipped and desperate.

Be rude. Don't shave. Drink too much on all occasions. (This is really a good one.)

Build a sauna bath in the garage.

Talk a lot about how you're thinking of trying STP.

Take up transcendental meditation.

Become an amateur etymologist.

Become an amateur painter.

Become an amateur photographer, ask your women friends to pose in the nude. When they do, make personal remarks.

This should get you off to a good start. You have established yourself in the eyes of all as a fellow worth knowing, and don't be surprised if a number of ladies suddenly indicate an interest in knowing you better. You are now negotiating from strength. All you have to do is decide which lady you should lavish all this splendor on.

Once you have made the choice, there are many approaches you can use. With most women, a few long looks at parties and a few surreptitious conversations in the kitchen about motorcycles or transcendental meditation are enough to get things rolling.

Some Approaches to Try
YOU ALONE CAN SAVE ME

This works particularly well if you have taken care to show previous signs of a secret sorrow. Far from repelling women, this kind of thing fascinates them. For women, whose nature is to comfort and console, are drawn as moths to the flame to the man nursing a mortal wound. Do your Humphrey Bogart act in the vicinity of the lady of your choice with determination until she is compelled to ask what it is all about. Let her work her way into your confidence—don't give in too easily—and eventually confess to her that, indeed, you have a secret sorrow. Invent here freely at your discretion.

Some good secret sorrows:

You have spent seventeen years in the advertising business and realize now that you are never going to write that novel.

Your son is about to be kicked out of Deerfield.

Your wife smokes pot.

Let her cheer you up—but not too much. You are launched.

THE CONFIDENCE GAME

Strangely enough, there are women who are timid and shy by nature and suspicious of the marauding male. Why any normal fellows would want any of these silly women is hard to understand, but they do, and if you do, too, here is how to go about it. Become great buddies with her and her husband. Issue some impromptu invitations—

spur-of-the-moment kind of thing—to her, in front of him. (The kind that she has to accept alone—such as the offer of a ride around the reservoir on the back of your motorcycle.) When he's out of town, invite her to dinner. But take her to a tea shop sort of restaurant, preferably one without a liquor license, and leave early, explaining that you have an important business engagement at eight-thirty. Look embarrassed. This should accomplish two ends: make her feel secure (you *have* a girlfriend), and simultaneously make her furious (you have a *girlfriend*). Start dropping over in the afternoon for stimulating conversation. Read to her out of Teilhard de Chardin. Bring along your butterfly collection so she can help you mount them. If you sense that she is still nervous, talk about your wife a lot. Refer to a mysterious secret love. Tell her you used to have a homosexual problem, but you think you're getting over it. This will make her even more secure and simultaneously even more furious. If you play your cards right, eventually she will pounce on you, out of sheer desperation.

THE HARPO MARX APPROACH

This is the simplest and most basic of all. Just walk boldly up to the lady of your choice, stare meaningfully into her eyes, and say, breathing heavily if you can manage it, "Gladys, I want you." Then grab her by the arm and drag her off.

Never mind corny. *It works.*

But over and over again, let us emphasize, that whether you worm your way into her confidence or attack with brute force, the secret is: Take her seriously.

Impress on the woman you have chosen that, great as your physical passion for her is, it is her mind that has captured you. An interesting corollary for women: The exact opposite works on men. Nothing is as heartwarming to the shy male as the confession that, stimulating as you find his conversation about the paper box industry, it's his hairy arms that turn you on.

Isn't nature wonderful?

WORDS TO LIVE BY

"The race is not always to the swift, but that is how to bet."

—GRANTLAND RICE

Some Opening Gambits—for Men and Women

The first move is always the hardest. Here are some safe and socially acceptable, you should forgive the expression, feelers.

1. The offer to help out: "I could come over Tuesday and put up the screens." "I'm *good* at scraping out dry rot." "I *love* simonizing motorcycles."

2. The mutual interest: "You mean *you* like underground movies *too?*"

3. Handholding: "Now this little bump here means you have an intensely passionate nature. How *about* that?"

4. The intensified social kiss: "Louise, your Yorkshire pudding was absolutely [grab, smooch] swell."

5. The straight proposition cloaked in humor: "Let's go down to the drive-in and neck in the back of the car." (If she [or he] doesn't laugh, you're in.)

CHAPTER FOUR

Logistics: Where to Go and How Often

HE IDEAL SITUATION FOR CREATIVE ADULTERY IS ONE IN WHICH ONE OR BOTH PARTNERS ARE AMPLY equipped with country houses, town houses, apartments in the city for business entertaining, châteaus in the south of France, caves overlooking the Aegean, and so forth. This allows for a high degree of mobility. However, not many are fortunate enough to have multiple domiciles available. The average adulterous couple has two—his and hers—and usually a spouse and several children in each, making things inconvenient all around. What to do? Here are some ideas.

The Hotel

If you are meeting in a distant city, a hotel is OK. But for steady rendezvous, conveniently near home, it is not really a good idea. First of all, it is expensive. Do not think you can save money by one of you booking a single room and the other sneaking up the fire stairs. Hotels *know*. And the truth about hotels is they don't care what you do, as long as you don't do it two for the price of one.

So you will have to book a double room. The hotel, with its numerous formalities, all those people you have to tip, and those maids that keep hovering around all morning waiting to come in and do the room, is a deterrent to a happy romantic assignation. True, there is room service—but this creates a timing problem, since in most hotels, the room waiter can arrive with the drinks, peanut butter sandwiches, or whatever, anywhere from ten minutes to four hours from the time you call him. Then he always wants to come back and get the dishes at the most inconvenient times.

Hotels are for married people. Tired old married people who keep regular hours. Besides, they think it's funny if you check in and stay for only two hours.

The Motel

The motel is, with the possible exception of the Pill, America's greatest contribution to the art of adultery. The anonymity of the parking lot entrances, self-service elevators, the absence of bellboys, to say nothing of hotel detectives, have made the motel rendezvous simple, convenient, and free from embarrassment. It is economical. You don't have to tip anybody. One of you can easily book a single room and wait for the other to stroll in through the back entrance. In fact, you can bring six friends. Motels are civilized and laissez-faire as long as you don't ask them to carry your luggage, don't break up the furniture, and don't throw beer bottles into the heated swimming pool. No problem about whether or not you have suitcases or how you sign the register. In a motel, you can sign Ursula Andress and Truman Capote, and no one will even notice.

Consider the many advantages of the wayside motel. Automatic coffee machines. The art on the walls—a different picture in every room. Oscillating chairs. (You didn't know about that, did you? Some of them even have oscillating beds.) What a pleasant setting for an afternoon meeting—a roadside motel room, its picture window overlooking the busy ebb and flow of life in the shopping center across the highway. The do-it-yourself charm of bringing your own bourbon and drinking it out of toothbrush glasses, with tap water and ice from the automatic ice dispenser down the hall. And perhaps a package of Fritos if anybody gets hungry. Then afterward, a quick workout in the vibrating chair, a quick dip in the heated swimming pool, and off on your separate ways with no one the wiser. The wayside motel, with its friendly flashing neon signs, the trucks roaring by at regular intervals, has been immortalized in literature as the setting for the romance of Humbert J. Humbert and his Lolita. The motel rendezvous is the American way of adultery.

His or Her House

Of course, the couple who really want to live dangerously can consider the possibility of meeting at his or her house. This has been accomplished successfully, particularly if the spouse is absent at given periods of time and can be counted on to stay away, but it is a risky business and we do not wholeheartedly recommend it. An unfortunate case we will cite is that of Agnes, who was married to a cello player. Every afternoon from two to five, her husband, Henry, was in the habit of practicing his cello in the basement. He had followed this pattern for fourteen years, so Agnes, when she began her liaison with Orville, felt reasonably secure in inviting him over in the afternoons. After all, what could happen as long as she could hear Henry going *voom voom voom* in the basement? However, she underestimated Henry, who, although a mite slow-witted, eventually became suspicious. Unbeknown to Agnes, Henry had a record made. *Voom, voom, voom.* Pow. Disaster.

So, we repeat, it is not a good idea to meet at his or her house. But if you do, take certain precautions. Do not leave your car or motorcycle outside the house. Leave it in the supermarket parking lot. Or in front of somebody else's house—that will confuse people. Always have a means of exit available. Back door. Window. Fire escape. Do not panic, if trapped, and do anything foolish, like hiding in the closet, under the bed, or crouched in a large wardrobe. This is tacky. It is best for the trapped visitor, if unknown to the returning spouse, to be introduced simply as the man from the Census Bureau, a representative of the Shady Acres Memorial Park, a RelaxAcisor saleslady, a political poll taker—be inventive. The spouse may wonder why you are so informally clothed but, it is hoped, be too polite to ask. Brazen it out.

If the partner is known to the returning spouse, try saying, "Hello Fred, good to see you. How's the old golf score?" or making some other appropriate greeting. Do not apologize. Do not explain. This may not work. But let's face it—what choice do you have?

The Borrowed Apartment

Borrowing someone's apartment is not recommended. If a man borrows an apartment from a single man friend—well, a single man is erratic. You cannot count on his being out of town when he says he will be; he is very likely to return at odd hours and then be annoyed with you, as if you were the one who goofed, not he. He will lend you the apartment and forget to tell you that is the day the cleaning woman is there, and the place is a shambles, with overflowing ashtrays, a sinkful of dishes, bed unmade and underwear strewn flamboyantly about. Not a place to bring a lady friend of taste and discrimination. On the other hand, when a man borrows an apartment from a single girl, nine times out of ten she's an old girlfriend, and she may *say* she's delighted to make life simpler for her successor, but she *isn't,* and somehow or other she will get back at the man. Like arranging to have somebody come fix the telephone on the appointed day. Or strewing crumbs in the bed. Women are just not good sports about this sort of thing.

The Pied-à-Terre

Of course, the serious adulterer sooner or later comes to the point at which he wishes to invest in a pad of his own. Like other sports—horseback riding, boating, or sky diving—that involve expensive equipment, it is wise to rent for a while, until you are sure you are serious about the pursuit. You do not buy a horse until you are sure your interest in galloping around the countryside every

Sunday morning is not going to wane. You do not buy a boat until you have learned a bit about what all those ropes are for and tried a few overnight excursions around Montauk Point. However, once you realize that the life on the ocean wave is for you, it is the expedient thing to invest in your own cruiser. The same with adultery. Motels are fine at first, but once you realize that adultery has become a way of life, the time has come to acquire a *pied-à-terre.*

Now, a *pied-à-terre* is not as formidable an undertaking as you might think. It means foot on the ground, and every respectable Frenchman in the golden age of adultery in France had one. It need not be expensive. Of course, it can be expensive, and if you are loaded, you can have a suite in the Waldorf Towers for a *pied-à-terre,* and good for you. But traditionally, the *pied-à-terre* is modest and charming. It is more romantic that way. A Presidential candidate and his lady, probably the most famous American adulterous couple of the early twentieth century, had their *pied-à-terre* in a simple brownstone (walk-up) in Greenwich Village. However, even this outlay isn't necessary.

In New York City, for example, if you can scrape up $45 or $50 a month, you can find a delightful little cold-water flat. Cold-water flat, in case you are not up on the ins and outs of poverty-line living in New York, used to mean hot water, but no heat. Now it means heat, too— but don't count on it. But you can have your love or an electric blanket (one that works on DC current) to keep you warm. Many a suburban commuter has built himself a little nest of this sort in the city, to which to retire for long lunch hours, the cocktail hour, or evenings when he's working late. You find them by walking around and looking for for-rent signs. Good neighborhoods—the *east* East Side, above Fiftieth Street (better *way* above); the fringes of Chelsea, the upper Lower East Side. The Village is too expensive; the West Side, too, since landlords are doing too thriving a business in packing in Puerto Rican families of seventeen into three rooms, at $25 a head a month.

The little fifth-floor walk-up you are likely to find will consist of perhaps two small rooms, railroad style, with a kitchen at one end and a bathtub in the kitchen. This may seem like an inconvenience, but think of the dramatic possibilities—she languishing in the bath, while he whips up his special caviar, onion, and sour cream sandwiches and feeds her little nibbles. (Of course, the corollary of the bathtub in the kitchen is the toilet in the hall, but you can't have everything.) Some of these apartments even have working fireplaces, but proceed with caution: Before you light one, no matter how cold the cold-water flat is, think of your picture in the *Daily News,* being carried down the ladder by a fireman attired only in your underwear and your electric blanket. However, fireplace or no, the place can be made very charming.

If you are not the homemaking type, don't *worry.* For some unknown reason, women are compulsive decorators. The unhandy man need only install the basic equipment. The ladies who visit him will instinctively start adding their own little touches, and after a series has done so, the bare little pad will flower into a veritable Bloomingdale's model room. A warning: Let only one lady decorate at a time. Don't let the next one start until the first one is out of your life. Women are not fools. Ingrid will know perfectly well it wasn't you who hung the birdcage full of paper flowers from the kitchen ceiling, and right away you're in trouble.

We have only given rules for establishing a *pied-à-terre* in New York, but the pattern, with some variations, can be followed in other cities. It doesn't have to be a cold-water flat. It can be two rooms over the Acme Garage. It is very important that your adulterous career be conducted in the proper surroundings. Environment is important. Automobiles, drive-in movies, and the like are all very well for teen-agers, but the adult adulterer needs a pad he can call his own.

How Often?

The successful adulterous relationship is best conducted on a regular schedule. It is not the frequency of meetings that is important; it is the fact that they are planned to occur at set times. This way, both parties can enjoy to the full the pleasure of anticipating, while ensuring as well that the affair does not interfere with other activities, such as going to work, keeping up a normal social life, or getting enough sleep. Your health is important.

Meetings can be scheduled, say, every Tuesday and Thursday, for dedicated couples who are serious about their hobby, or as infrequently as once a year, during the Lumber and Plywood Management Association Convention. Quality, not quantity, is the watchword here. Plan ahead. Of course, the occasional surprise phone call or impromptu visit can be delightful, but old spur-of-the-moment, drop-in Charlie, who makes a practice of calling at 2 A.M. and announcing that he just happens to be in

town or just up the street, and so on, is not handling
things well at all. (See Advice to Singles, page 61.) Nor
is the fellow (or girl) whose idea of an impromptu
rendezvous is sneaking away in the middle of the country
club dance or dropping by the house on Sunday morning
while his partner's spouse is off getting the newspapers or
taking the kids to Sunday school. This kind of behavior is
unsettling, irresponsible, and leads only to disaster. Step
one in planning an adulterous career is to get a long
yellow pad and plenty of nice sharp pencils and to draw
up a regular schedule.

When to Meet and Why

Tuesdays and Thursdays: for a stable relationship.
Every other Wednesday: to keep the franchise.
Breakfast: if you're overbooked.
Lunch: if you're dieting.
Cocktail hour: if you've just joined Alcoholics Anonymous.
Constantly: if you trying to give up smoking.
Nonsked: if you're scared.
Fourth of July: if you're a good American.
Millard Fillmore's birthday: why not?

Where to Go and Why

Motel: convenience and anonymity.
His house: brinkmanship.
Her house: Russian roulette.
Beach: sunshine.
Back of car: desperation.

Front of car: masochism.
Plaza Hotel: gracious living.
Mount Everest: because it's there.
Drive-in movie: cultural enrichment.
Schrafft's: kicks.
Yellowstone National Park: see America first.

Things to Say If Cornered

"I'm only seeking my identity."
"It's a form of social protest."
"I hate myself."
"It must have been the Methedrine."
"You have no sense of humor."
"I'm making an underground movie."
"I didn't like it."
"I hated it."
"I'm trying to give up smoking."
"I love you."
"This *isn't* Cleveland?"

CHAPTER FIVE

Combinations and How They Work

N THIS CHAPTER, WE WILL TAKE UP THE VARIOUS ADULTEROUS COMBINATIONS THAT ARE POSSIBLE, THEIR advantages and drawbacks, and how they can be made to work for you.

Two Married People

The best possible adulterous relationship, as we have pointed out before, is between two happily married people. There are reasons for this. Both are negotiating from a position of strength. Each has something to fall back on. Neither wishes to create a disaster. Equilibrium can be maintained.

One happily and one unhappily married person is not an impossible situation. In fact, the support and example afforded the unhappily married partner by the happily married one may strengthen or even save the failing marriage.

Two unhappily married people? This hardly ever works. These two are going to hate each other as much as they hate their respective spouses.

Remember: There is no such thing as an unhappy marriage. There are only unhappy people.

Single Woman, Married Man

This is the classic adulterous situation. Men have had mistresses since time began, and it is an honorable institution.

It is a well-known sociological fact that the mistress lends stability to family life. Consider the example of the French. Or take the Japanese, well known for family solidarity, filial obedience, and a genius for manufacturing cheap cameras. This is all directly attributable to the institution of the Geisha.

However, the mistress of the past, despite her enviable situation and real contribution to society, lacked freedom and social position. Today's career mistress, who may be an executive secretary, account supervisor, or child psychologist, is economically independent and can tell Henry to shove it if she feels like it. Which makes the situation more intriguing and also a lot cheaper for Henry.

(Of course, there is a large army of single women who *pretend* an interest in adultery because they think they can trap the man into marrying them. These women do not have the true vocation and married men are advised to steer clear of them. They are nothing but trouble.) The great advantage of the single woman-married man combination is that you have a place to go. She has her own apartment, and her time is freer. She can usually arrange long business lunches; she can also be dropped in on early in the morning or at the cocktail hour.

Also, entertaining expenses are at a minimum, considering the possibilities of little candlelit dinners (Career mistresses always want to cook you little candlelit dinners.

Sometimes they also want to hang onto your socks and darn them too, but watch out—that way disaster lies.) In any case, in liquor bills alone, the single career mistress is an asset to the economy-minded adulterer.

The disadvantages of the situation are: (1) that she may start nudging you to get a divorce and marry her (see above) and (2) that she will see other men. This (2) is sadly unavoidable. If it happens, be philosophical; fair is fair. If you can divide your affections, so can she.

From the woman's point of view, there are many advantages to this situation. The average woman has been conditioned to believe that it is a mistake to take up with a married man because he cannot marry her. What a silly point of view! The obvious advantage of her taking up with a married man is that she does not have to marry him. Also, she is obviously justified in having more than one.

Single Man, Married Woman

This can be, if handled properly, one of the most beautiful of all emotional relationships. Think of the possibilities. There are many young men around, earnest, dedicated types who reason that they may never become the new Dr. Albert Schweitzer, Norman Mailer, Andy Warhol, or whoever it is they aspire to be, if they burden themselves with a wife and family. So they settle for a career of discreet alliances with other people's wives. This arrangement also solves the problem of where to go. The single man usually has his own apartment. Of course, he is not so likely to cook little candlelit dinners (if he does, watch out), but she is. Even if she has a cook to cook them at home. Especially if she has a cook to cook them at home. She is also inclined to start fixing up the place.

In allying himself with a married woman, not only does the single man get a free cook and decorator, but he is also lavished with love and affection by a woman wise in the ways of the world, whose demands on his time are minimal, since she must budget her hours with him carefully—*and* who is supported by somebody else. It may seem that the single man is getting the better of the bargain. But no. Consider it from the woman's point of view. She has, let's face it, nothing much to do all day. So, instead of opening a paper dress boutique in New Canaan or something dumb like that, she arranges to spend her time with a charming, intelligent, vital young man, who is her adoring slave. (It is very easy to be an adoring slave if it's only on alternate Tuesdays and Fridays.)

Her ego is restored, her youth recaptured. She can get great satisfaction out of knowing that she is the inspiration behind his kinetic sculpture or pornographic poetry, without actually having to live on the proceeds.

The single man who takes up with a married woman is likely to be younger. Why this happens, we don't know— maybe it's because single men *are* younger. In some cases, he will be much, *much* younger—and this can be a splendid relationship, if the older woman approaches it in the proper spirit.

The Much, Much Younger Man

A drawback of the much, *much* younger man is that he often does not have a charming little pad of his own—he lives in some kind of dormitory or, worse, with his mother. But this need not be a problem. Since he has no money to spend on his married lady friend, he will generally offer to do little things for her, like explain the theories of Herbert Marcuse, tutor her in Swahili or build a sleeping deck in the upstairs study, depending on his particular talents. This also nicely solves the problem of where to go, as long as he keeps conjugating Swahili verbs, if that's what you do with Swahili verbs, or hammering, while her husband is home. His presence is easily explained as "that nice young man who is a friend of Cousin Charlie's Edna who is working his way through graduate school giving Swahili lessons." And what husband could suspect that Edna's boyfriend, for heaven's sake, could be interested in a woman his wife's age? (Ha.)

There are pitfalls inherent in the older-married-woman-single-younger-man relationship, and here they are. First, do not think about the age difference. Remember what Dr. Kinsey said: Women are at their peak at thirty-five and men at nineteen. He may be too old for you already. Do not be dismayed if you find out he took Edna to the movies. She may be eighteen years old and a dead ringer for Mia Farrow, but what does she *know*? And not only about Swahili verbs. Think positive. Remember, you have a lifetime of experience, wit, worldly wisdom, and charm to offer this boy. If your husband should make rude remarks—such as "I think Edna's boyfriend has a crush on you, Mother"—don't be unhappy. Smile secretly to yourself. After all, he's not exactly Sonny Wisecarver himself.

Do not be tempted, as many older women are, to lavish him with gifts. No gold cigarette cases or Sulka ties. First of all, his friends will wonder where he got them and suspect him of all sorts of strange things, like connections with the Mafia. Do not be tempted, for example, to pay his way through graduate school. Let him keep on giving Swahili lessons—it's good for his character. He loves you for yourself alone. Quit while you're ahead.

CHAPTER SIX

Advice to Singles

LTHOUGH THIS BOOK IS PRIMARILY FOR MARRIED PEOPLE, WE ARE NOT OVERLOOKING SINGLES. THEY, TOO, can profit from the theory of horizontal enrichment.

The trouble with most single people is that they are obsessed with the idea of marriage. You would think, considering some of the marriages they observe about them, that they might be somewhat disenchanted, but no.

They hurl themselves into a feverish round of activities designed to bring them into contact with other single people, just as desperate as themselves. Singles weekends in the Catskills. Bachelor cruises. Over twenty-eight clubs. They stalk each other, measure each other, try to fake each other out—procedures that are not only depressing, but totally nonconducive to romance. They spend a lot of time going to psychiatrists.

However, once a single person decides to accept his singleness—forsakes his friends at Maxwell's Plum, removes his name from the rolls of the computer date bureau—once he admits, that is, that marriage is not the only goal, all sorts of new and exciting possibilities open up.

Instead of the dreary crowd down at the singles bar, he can choose among a whole new group of partners, who just happen to be married to other people. Charming, delightful partners who wouldn't be caught dead on a bachelor cruise, who are as bored with the married state as he is with the single and are eager to work out appropriate arrangements to the advantage of both. And what a refreshing change for the single person! These new married friends do not think of him as one of society's rejects (as he, indeed, comes to think of himself after a couple of go-rounds with singles-only social groups). Quite the contrary. They see him as a glamorous, independent, fun-loving participant in a mysterious and exciting world that they are somehow barred from. They see him as a swinger. Wouldn't you *rather* be a swinger? Of course you would. Then what is the problem?

Being the single half of a married-single combination has much to recommend it. (See Combinations and How They Work, page 53), but there are, of course, traps. The first and most obvious trap is the temptation to start once again thinking in terms of marriage. Many single people enter a liaison intending to observe the rules of the game, and then weaken, and start whining and complaining because their married friend will not get a divorce and marry them. This sort of thing has, in fact, given singles a bad name, and many married people avoid liaisons with them for this reason. Don't be a fink. Play by the rules. Do your part to demonstrate that singles want no special privileges and, if given the opportunity, can compete in every way on an equal footing with marrieds.

To do this successfully, the single must have an *other thing*. They have their home life (swell), and you have your *other thing*—preferably another romance; if not, some special project: writing a novel, practicing tap dancing, studying computer programming, and so on. If you don't actually have any *other thing* at the moment, get one. Without some nice, distracting *other thing,* you're apt to get grabby or nasty or weepy and spoil everything.

Of course, sometimes it is the married person who will get grabby and spoil everything—if you let him. A type that can make life very difficult for the single girl is the man with the caliph complex.

Some men are forever trying to set up a harem. It's a fantasy they've had from childhood. They *will* keep at it, like beavers building dams, no matter how complicated it gets. It's an instinct. You can recognize the man with a true caliph complex. He immediately tries to establish you as his alone. This means, simply, that he wants both you *and* his wife (though he will explain to you at enormous length that there's no true affection between them anymore) to be faithful and true blue.

If you remark on the unfairness of this arrangement, he will make a great big fuss and throw a jealous fit and try to wrap it all up by suggesting that if you just have a little patience and faith, the very minute the youngest of his nine children graduates from college (the kid is only six, mind), he will marry you, whom he loves above all others.

What he would like is to have you around every Thursday at lunch and every Friday evening when he's supposed to be at the gin rummy club. And the rest of the time you should stay home and study algebra. He tends to call around eleven in the evening every once in a while to say "I love you more than Hershey Bars." This is very touching and dear, but he's really checking to see that you're home.

Some married people set up a one-way communications system. They can call you anytime, but you can't call them. You must equalize this arrangement. Start by letting the phone ring once in a while. Many eternal optimists, convinced that there's nothing but yum-yums at the other end of the line, simply can't bear to let a phone go unanswered. Build character. Let it ring.

If you really can't stand it, get an answering service. This way you can pick up the phone (quietly!), listen to who's calling, and then decide whether you want to talk to him.

"Where were you at twelve o'clock last night when I called?"

"Oh, home, of course, but I didn't feel like answering the phone."

Establish definite times and places where you can call them. Don't write letters. (Don't, it's really scary.) But anyone too chicken to take an occasional phone call at his office deserves to remain monogamous.

Discourage the drop-in or hi y-aal system right from the start. The drop-in can keep you in a constant state of nervous suspension, and besides, it makes it very hard for you to carry on with anyone *else*. The next time Darling Grace or Cheerful Charlie appears unannounced, send her or him packing and say that this is the night you watch *Star Trek* on TV. Total availability is bad for your image, and you *could* just have someone peacefully napping in your bed at the moment. So if you make it quite clear that drop-ins are unwelcome, you will never have to cope with any situations too ghastly to contemplate.

Once you've established your independence, you'll be amazed at how people fall in line. Maurice's wife will appreciate you all the more because you've established your manhood, and a whisper of jealousy won't hurt *her* any.

Clarence with the caliph complex will say that the twentieth century is a rotten century, and women don't know how to behave anymore. They've lost the spirit of true femininity; two hundred years ago he'd have traded eight camels for you, and that would have been that. If he's truly Orient-oriented, he may pack his caravan and look elsewhere, but most likely he'll be absolutely fascinated with your thousand and one devious excuses and keep coming back for more.

Remember that the great advantage of singleness is freedom. Freedom from responsibility. Freedom from having to account to anyone about anything. Freedom to go out with other people if you like. Don't lose it. Let your married friends count on you, but not completely.

RULES TO LIVE BY

1. You need more than one partner; otherwise you'll start taking the whole thing too seriously.
2. Better if they live out of town—way out.
3. Never give *anybody* a key.

CHAPTER SEVEN

Occupational Hazards

HIS CHAPTER IS DIRECTED AT WOMEN ONLY. THERE IS NO COMPARABLE CHAPTER FOR MEN, BECAUSE women are relative newcomers to the business and professional worlds and no significant body of data exists. Besides, they all are trying very hard, and any top-of-the-head observations about the peculiarities of lady physicists or lady real estate operators might be unnecessarily discouraging at this point in history.

Doctors: Doctors are difficult to cope with in adulterous situations because they are difficult to get hold of in any situation. The busy and dedicated man of medicine has a hard enough time fitting his patients into his round of social activities, let alone you. So doctors are, generally speaking, a poor choice. With one exception. Did you know that of all medical specialists, pediatricians have the busiest extramarital life? The reason is absurdly simple: They make house calls, and the lady isn't sick.

Lawyers: Lawyers, on the other hand, are a good choice. Genial, jolly companions, they are skilled in the arts of subterfuge and making things seem what they are not, so that there is little danger of getting caught. And if you are, you have, of course, a smart lawyer. If your own marital scene is in any way tricky, having a lawyer as a lover is an excellent way of combining pleasure with business.

Psychiatrists: This can be good or bad, depending on how fond you are of self-examination. A psychiatrist can provide a running commentary on the affair in progress that will either: (1) provide you with a needed sense of self-justification or (2) drive you absolutely crackers. Proceed at your own risk.

Clergymen: A very rewarding area. Do not be put off by clerical garb or pious stance. We read much these days about the "swinging clergy." This is nothing new. Look back a little—Pope Julian IV, Peter Abelard, John Donne, the Reverend Arthur Dimmesdale, Henry Ward Beecher, Elmer Gantry—clergymen have always been great lovers. Contemporary clergymen, anxious as they are to cast off the yoke of centuries, to come to terms with the secular world and generally to change the corporate image, not only tend to go in for the joys of the flesh, but think they invented them. You may be getting more than you bargained for.

Businessmen: The ranks and gradations of the techno-structure are a perfectly grand place to look for a partner. Black Power, Italian Power, Flower Power, and so on are all very well and good, but there's nothing like Power Power to make a girl feel secure, and here is where it lies. The best place to look is middle and upper-middle management. Above or below that, they are generally too busy: (1) Getting There or (2) Staying There to have too much time for you. But middle management—here we combine prestige, high salaries, large expense accounts, a good deal of traveling (they go to conventions in Puerto Rico a lot) and (trade secret) nothing, really, to do. Consequently, lots of time for the most elaborate kinds of fun and games.

Public Servants: Those in public office have many of the advantages of business executives—high mobility, lots of traveling, no visible work. They do not have much in the way of expense accounts—the government is notoriously chintzy in this respect—but of course, there is always graft. They can take you traveling, although it is more likely on a fact-finding mission to Pitcairn Island than to Puerto Rico. They do have a built-in cop-out, of course—"While I'm running for office, Hazel, I'm afraid we'll have to cool it"—but don't be put off. Cite the known liaisons of any of our most distinguished statesmen. History is on your side.

Creative Types: Writers, composers, painters, actors, and so on are strictly for masochists. They are charming, entertaining, good to look at, take you fascinating places, and have a good deal of cachet among the more impressionable ("You don't mean *the* Ed Sullivan?"), but in the long run they love only themselves. They have to. It is the nature of their business. So, unless you really like being either Big Mama or Little Miss Doglike Devotion, forget it.

Academics: There was a time when a schoolteacher was a sensitive young man who would come over on Saturday afternoon and read to you out of Walter Savage Landor. No more. (In fact, try to find one who has even heard of Walter Savage Landor.) Today's schoolteacher is a heads-up go-getter, bucking for associate professor, assistant dean, or whatever the next step up the ladder is. He spends his days apple-polishing and his nights taking courses in fund raising. He can be entertaining if you get him talking about his discipline, but usually all he wants to talk about is how he knocked them dead at the American Entomologists Convention where those cats from Berkeley were really giving him the hard once-over. Or, how much he's taking Redi-Ded Exterminators, Inc., for in consulting fees. Today's academic is out to make it big. If he does, of course, he enjoys all the advantages of the executive, plus the fact that he has free access to foundation money for every conceivable purpose.

A Quick Checklist of Whom to Pick and Why

Simple sex: research physicist.

Sex and dancing: businessman from the Midwest.

Sex and conversation: undergraduate from CCNY.

Sex and skiing: psychiatrist.

Sex and a college education: philosophically inclined longshoreman.

Sex and cultural stimulation: dentist.

Sex and travel: Peace Corps volunteer.

Sex and mental health: public relations man.

Sex and high living: union leader.

Sex and politics (right wing): movie actor.

Sex and politics (left wing): television actor.

Sex and drinking: Presbyterian clergyman.

Sex and pot: middle-aged literary critic.

Sex and gourmet cooking: manager of A&P.

CHAPTER EIGHT

Cross-Cultural Adultery

THNIC DIVERSITY IS WHAT HAS MADE AMERICA GREAT, AND ETHNIC DIVERSITY CAN ADD NEW RICHNESS and dimension to your adulterous career. However, there are pitfalls inherent in relationships with all the major religious and ethnic groups.

There was a time when discussing these matters was called bigotry, but these days, if you keep up with the popular (and unpopular) press, you will find all kinds of nasty name-calling going on. Only it is not called bigotry anymore; it is called sociology. (Jewish mothers, indeed! We could tell you about some Jewish *sons,* but never mind.) So. A few sociological notes.

Watch out for Catholics. Especially you ladies who have been brought up on the "my wife is a Catholic, so I can't get a divorce" bit. Ha. You do not know the New Catholics. Divorce is *in.* They all want to get divorces. Do not be trapped into divorce and remarriage by some Catholic who wants to prove how broad-minded he or she is. Also, if your Catholic friend is in any way intellectual, he will be very left-wing. So study up on the writings of Chairman Mao.

Jews are not terribly good at adultery, because more than any other group they are hung up on the Protestant ethic. Why this should be so is a mystery, but then we are not theologians, but simple reporters. However, if your

Jewish lady or gentleman friend has strong moral reservations about what he or she is doing, don't worry unduly. Probably there is a psychiatrist in the offing who is busily resolving this dilemma, taking a lot of the burden off you.

Protestant is a hard category to pin down, since many people these days who are supposed to be Protestants, if asked their religion, will answer agnostic, Buddhist, don't know, etc., or will tell you they believe in world fellowship. Anybody who calls himself a Protestant is probably either Harvey Cox or the religion editor of *Time* magazine, and dealing with these types is beyond the scope of this book. Conventional Protestants (Baptists, Methodists, etc.) are apt to be a bit sticky about adultery. This is not because of the Protestant ethic, which they never heard of, but because of how it looks. However, once nobody is looking, watch out. Especially for Episcopalians; they are the worst kind.

It is very fashionable to have cross-color-line affairs, and they can be most rewarding to both parties, but there can be problems. Women are advised to watch out for Black Power politicians. Their cause may be an exciting one, but like any other political movement, it tends to bog down into bureaucracy, and your friend may spend so much time at strategy meetings, conferences with Henry Ford II, and TV panel discussions that you can only keep track of him by watching the eleven o'clock news—alone. Besides, don't forget you're dealing with male supremacists, and if you get told to wipe off your makeup or let down your miniskirt—well, we warned you. And any man who thinks he is getting some sort of sex kitten in a black girl can generally forget it. The next thing you know you will find yourself out distributing campaign literature while she runs for the state senate. Blacks should watch out for white types as categorized by religion above, with one more across-the-board pitfall: They are all likely to spend a great deal of time talking about the Movement—if, in fact, they do not wish to take it over, working, of course, through you. In any case, prepare yourself for a lot of long, earnest discussions and self-examinations about collective guilt, which can get tedious.

CHAPTER NINE

Dangerous Partners, or Types to Watch Out for

HERE ARE SOME PEOPLE WHO ARE JUST NOT CUT OUT FOR A SUCCESSFUL CAREER IN HORIZONTAL ENrichment. They lack the proper attitude. This is usually not just a case of misguided behaviors, but a deep-seated character defect.

Study the categories below. If your partner or contemplated partner fits into one, be warned. If you note these tendencies in yourself, adultery is not for you. Stay married, stay single, but in any case, stay out of the game. Don't spoil things for the serious players.

The Demanding Woman: She doesn't demand marriage (often because she *is* already married), but she demands. Sometimes it's tangible proof of affection in the form of merchandise—a little emerald-eyed tiger from David Webb, a sable jumpsuit from Revillon, a powder-blue Aston-Martin—all of which she says she can attribute at home to the indulgence of her Great-Aunt Harriet. Possibly worse is the lady who demands less tangible things. Such as the lady who reasons: "I am having an affair with Walter because my own husband, Arthur, spends his evenings refinishing furniture in the cellar and never talks to me. Besides, he never buys me presents

70

except on Christmas, my birthday, and our wedding anniversary." Consequently, this lady demands that Walter spend hours at a time talking to her; this tends to take up a lot of the time Walter has allotted for other pursuits. She casts baleful glances at him because he doesn't buy her presents, although she doesn't tell him it's because he doesn't buy her presents—she expects him to *know*. Consequently, friction develops, arguments, recriminations, and so forth, until Walter decides: Who needs it? Adultery is supposed to be a *fun* relationship. Arguments he can get at home.

The Loser: From the moment he first grasps your little hand he starts to brood about when he will lose you. Now he hasn't really got you yet, so this may be a bit unnerving. As time goes on, he will drop into the conversation deadening little sentences like "Eventually you'll get bored with me." You hadn't thought of it yet, but well . . . "George [your husband] looks like a champion tennis player." You hadn't noticed George's looks much at all for the last eleven years, but now that he mentions it . . . He will run on through "You're too good for me"; "What do you see in me?"; "My hair is thinning"; "Do you think I'm too fat?" If you can still stand him after all that, he will start to push you by calling eight times a day and maybe picking little quarrels. "You were three minutes late yesterday; obviously you don't love me." So long.

The Winner: The winner sees life as one big crap game. He—sometimes she—will have to have read more books than you, traveled more places (if not, appreciated them more), have more money (or less, because money is rotten), know more interesting people, be a better judge of wine, etc., etc. Point of all this is that lucky you have been personally selected to be the Love Object (isn't it astounding?) by wonderful HIM. Champion winners often wonder why they spend so much time alone. It's because they win so quickly. When you meet a winner, shake hands, clap him on the shoulder, say, "Congratulations! You win," and depart.

The Split Personality: He does, and he doesn't. He will, and he won't. He wants to philander—he's fascinated by the idea. He is simultaneously scared, guilt-ridden, feels that what he is doing is wrong (afterward) and is constantly taking secret vows never to do *that* again.

His problem is that he wants to be simultaneously a swinger and a pillar of virtue. He operates with the fine logic of a bank robber who feels morally obligated to report his take to the Internal Revenue Service.

He finds a nice compliant single lady (a married one would require too much planning, and he's not up to that) and falls in love. Now you would think that being in love would inspire him to behave properly. But no. That fact in itself is supposed to be enough for her. That and a surprise visit every time fancy strikes. (To him adultery, like murder, isn't so bad if it's unpremeditated.) He tells her he may call next Wednesday, when he's in town for the annual meeting of the Apple Growers Association. So next Wednesday she cancels her creative writing class, cooks a cunning little casserole just in case, chills some wine, and, of course, no show. Then, a week later, just as she settles down for a peaceful evening at home with her hair up in rollers, guess who calls to say she can have him for four whole hours. The obvious countermove for ladies here is to be, firmly, otherwise occupied when the surprise phone call comes. But it doesn't really work. If she tries it, the Split Personality is surprised, mystified, and wounded. What did he do wrong? Then he does it again.

The Detective: The Detective has to know every detail of your life. Whether you're Scorpio or Pisces. Blood type. Names and ages of all your children. How you proposed to Grace/Henry. What you read on the train, eat for breakfast, whether you use a hard or soft toothbrush. Does she care about your opinion on the Middle East? No. She wants to know where you buy your shorts. Does she want to hear the latest Italian joke? No. She wants to know where you were last Friday at 11:15 P.M. Sooner or later all these questions are going to make you nervous, and in self-defense you'll begin to lie. "I was at the movies, and I have twelve witnesses." "Roberta and I eloped to Haiti and had a wedding performed by a voodoo priest." "Our children don't have names, only numbers—One, Two, Three, Four. . . ." One way to get out of this one is to call her and say you've been arrested on a morals charge and the police are looking for her, too, and she better leave town quickly.

The Lady Novelist: In her creative writing class, the Lady Novelist has been taught to write about what she *knows*—and this may well turn out to be you. Now every prudent adulterer knows that letter writing is a large mistake to begin with, but this doesn't stop the Lady Novelist. (Little short of perhaps strangling does.) She will insist on writing you letters. If you manage to dissuade her from sending them to your home or office, she will write them anyway and hand them to you. Quite good letters, usually with long descriptive passages about the weather, her mood, the charming little incident she observed today and how it reminded her of you. Next, when you say something she considers worthy, she may exclaim, "Oh, that's marvelous—I must write it down." This is the time to shut up and maybe even leave for a tour of the Greek islands, for everything is grist for her mill. Otherwise, you will find yourself all written up (in excruciating detail) in Chapter 11.

The Confessor: The Confessor is a very, *very* dangerous type. If things start to go wrong or his conscience starts to bother him, the first thing he does is run off and tell someone all about it. Someone like his wife or your husband. If he were satisfied with telling his dentist or psychiatrist, it might be all right, but no, he has to tell *Gertrude*.

"I have to be honest," he will explain with that smug, virtuous look you never did like. So good old honest Henry goes and tells tolerant, understanding Gertrude. Well, she's so tolerant and understanding that after she throws her glass of red wine all over Henry's new Cardin suit and says she'll never have you (not him, *you*) in the house again as long as she lives, she feels better, and when he promises with tears and all that he loves her best and will never do it again, ever, ever, and he doesn't know what came over him, she forgives him. So everything's just swell with Henry and Gertrude (except for the suit), but she never invites you and George over for dinner anymore, and George is beginning to wonder why.

What Henry is is not an adult adulterer at all, but an emotional sadist out for a little long-term revenge. For him, getting caught is half the fun. He's really trying to get back at Gertrude for all the years she kept saying things like "Actions speak louder than words" or "Live and let live" to him. He's not only living a little, but also giving her a little loud action as well, and how about that, Gertie Baby?

You can detect this type early. He will mumble, when you're coziest, "I really shouldn't be here." Or tell you how madly in love he was with his last girlfriend. Or write letters. He wants documents, which means, subconsciously, he wants to be caught and enjoy all the hell that will break loose.

The Lady Confessor: She suddenly gets mad because it's St. Swithin's Day and you forgot to send her a card and St. Swithin's Day is the anniversary of the day you stopped for your first cup of coffee at Danny's Diner for God's sake. So she calls your wife and says, "Hello, my name is Alice, and you don't know me, but . . ."

When you get home from the office, you find all your bags packed and set out on the stoop, and all your wife will say is "Who's Alice?" boringly, over and over, and your head hurts and you can't remember who Alice is and you are in Bad Trouble.

Of course, it's all over with Alice—even she has begun to realize this by now, and she's crying because of what she's *done*—but you are faced with the problem of getting all your bags back in the house and unpacked.

(Alices are recognizable because they're (1) single so nothing can happen to them and (2) very dumb. Watch out for dumb girls. They also get pregnant and call you at the office a lot.)

Gents of a Lower Station in Life: This is usually a mistake. Unlike the celebrated Lady Chatterley, you'll find it pretty dull. No conversation except a lot of ruminating about will the Mets win the pennant. Or he'll try to impress you by telling you he reads the *New Yorker*. Furthermore, he'll boast to the other guys at the supermarket.

(Though D. H. Lawrence never mentioned it, it is a well-known fact that after the bewhiskered gamekeeper frolicked with Lady Chatterley in the garden with the flowers and all, he hotfooted it right off to the local pub, where, grinning broadly over his porter, he told the boys, "I done it wi' the missus.")

CHAPTER TEN

Four Cautionary Tales: Some Case Histories

EAD THESE SAD CASE HISTORIES. DO YOU SEE YOURSELF IN ANY OF THEM?

Case I: Lucy and Hubert

Lucy and Hubert met each other at a Unitarian Young Marrieds Cookout, which both attended without their respective spouses, and Hubert offered Lucy a ride home on the back of his motorcycle. They discovered an affinity and soon were meeting regularly every other Wednesday at a motel in the next township. This arrangement cheered Lucy, who had been pretty bored as things were, immensely.

Suddenly, life regained it savor. Indeed, it regained so much savor that Lucy decided this was the great romance of all time and that she and Hubert should get divorces and marry. Hubert had also been cheered up by the arrangement but was not at all cheered up when Lucy began suggesting and then demanding marriage. The great romance of all time didn't, in his mind, justify his having to support two wives and seven children, to say nothing of the expenses involved and wear and tear on all concerned. Besides, his wife, Isabel, had also been the

77

great romance of all time at one point, and he had been through that one and out the other end. Well, this led to tears and scenes and finally an impasse, in which Lucy said such awful things to Hubert's secretary for not letting her talk to Hubert (on Hubert's orders, of course) that the girl quit. She also went around telling everybody in town entertaining stories about Lucy and Hubert, and of course, it got back to Isabel, who did not find it so entertaining. Total disaster for all.

How much better for all—Lucy, George (that's Lucy's husband), Isabel, Hubert, and Hubert's secretary (who has been unemployed for a good long time, because who wants a secretary who tells all, no matter how entertaining it is?)—had Hubert and Lucy just gone on meeting at the motel and growing old gracefully together every other Wednesday. For now, indeed, both Hubert and Lucy are divorced, although it was not their idea this time. Hubert is happily married to another woman eleven years younger than Lucy, and Lucy is going to therapy group every other Wednesday to find out why men are so rotten.

Case II: Dorothy and Walter

Dorothy, an appealing young woman with a trusting look, great wistful eyes, a lovely six-bedroom house in the suburbs, a summer house, four adorable children, and an independent income, caught the attention of Walter (as well she might), not, however, because of the afore-mentioned assets, but because she seemed so unhappy.

When she confided in Walter that despite her surface happiness, she was miserable because her husband didn't love her, Walter, a jolly, generous type, who was kind to children and took in stray cats, decided something should be done about that. Fortunately, it was summer, and Dorothy was installed in the country house, so at some expense to his business (which was installing kitchen equipment) he managed to take a day or two off in mid-week and visit Dorothy in Bucks County. (They were installing a lot of kitchens in Bucks County that year.)

This was a happy arrangement for a while; then Dorothy became querulous. She started saying Walter didn't love her after all. His wife was so much prettier than she, Dorothy, that how could he love her? Now Walter's wife, Mildred, was an admirable woman in many ways, but Elizabeth Taylor she wasn't. Walter assured Dorothy that she was much prettier than Mildred, ever so much, with those big brown eyes and darling little figure, and this placated her. But only for a while. The next week she was troubled again. "Mildred is so much more *capable* than I am. You can't possibly love me."

Walter assured her putting up six dozen jars of peach chutney and three dozen jars of green tomato relish every summer was nice if you like peach chutney and green tomato relish, but Dorothy had other good qualities. What? Dorothy wanted to know, citing Mildred's intelligent conversation, firm hand with children, and natural qualities of leadership, as evidenced the time the PTA of which she was president locked horns with the board of education. With all that going for Mildred, how could he love her? Furthermore, she knew he didn't really want to drive all that way out to the country, and he was doing it just because he felt sorry for her; furthermore she had had one cold after another all summer long, and she knew perfectly well he found this unattractive; furthermore, her children were such a bunch of screaming brats and must get on his nerves; furthermore, the refrigerator in the country house kept going out of whack, and she didn't know how to fix it, which must be a great trial to a man in the kitchen equipment business.

After many weeks it began to come through to Walter that Mildred was indeed capable, intelligent, a good mother, had natural qualities of leadership, wasn't too bad-looking, never had colds, and besides, she didn't natter all the time. So he told Dorothy that the kitchen business was at its seasonal high and required his full attention, went home, and stayed home. From time to time he missed Dorothy but made up for his loss by taking in another stray cat.

Dorothy is a classic rejectee. She said, "Kick me," to Walter so many times that eventually he kicked her. Perhaps she wanted it that way all along; who knows? Doubtless that was her problem with her husband and will be the problem with other men in the future. Poor Dorothy!

(Dorothy is a true loser, but there is one type even worse, that men would do well to watch out for, and that is the *faux* loser. This is the girl whose every attitude says, "Kick me," and when her harassed partner, following the by this time irresistible urge, raises his foot to kick her—*pow*. Right where it counts. Watch out for this deceptive type.)

Case III: Herb and Phoebe

Herb, an exemplary husband and father of five, suffers from what we call the Suburban Husband Syndrome.

That is, he is confused about his self-image. On the other hand, he chases women; this proves that he is a swinger. Then when he catches them, he nobly abandons them; this proves his moral superiority.

Herb, in his swinger manifestation, set about pursuing Phoebe, a simple, trusting type in the steno pool in his office. Their first date should have been a warning to Phoebe about what was coming: He arranged to meet her in a delightful little Italian restaurant at seven-thirty. Well, after Phoebe waited for forty-five minutes, sitting on a very uncomfortable little chair near the door because they wouldn't let unescorted women sit at the bar, she got a phone call from Herb, saying he couldn't meet her; he had to go home because one of his children was running a temperature. Well, OK.

The next evening they met, had a delightful dinner, and retired to Phoebe's apartment. During the next week and a half, Herb dropped by Phoebe's place almost every night, and a good time was had by all. Herb protested his undying love for Phoebe, and Phoebe, after a while, began protesting total exhaustion. But, a philosophical type, she observed that it beat watching television. Then there was a week's silence from Herb, after which he started calling again. Then, after two months' silence, he called again at 11 P.M. and came over. He explained to Phoebe that he hadn't been around because of a crisis in his office, but it was over now, and he still loved her madly. They made a date for dinner the following Wednesday, which Herb broke at the last minute, because his brother arrived unexpectedly from Minneapolis. The next week he came by her apartment four times, and the last time he told her he was getting a divorce, and would she marry him? Phoebe thought this was odd, but then it isn't every day a vice-president in charge of Midwestern market analysis asks you to marry him. Silence for two weeks, and then Herb called her to ask if he could come over for a serious conversation.

The serious conversation went like this: "Phoebe," said Herb sternly, "I have decided to give you up."

"*Nu* so?" said Phoebe.

"Basically," said Herb, "I'm a decent fellow. A relationship like this goes against the grain with me. I feel guilty all the time, and I can't stand what the tension it's causing might do to my family. I mean, I'm probably giving the kids all kinds of traumas. After all, Phoebe, I'm a married man."

"Has anybody been saying you were single?" Phoebe murmured as she closed the door after the retreating Herb. For a moment she entertained the thought of paying a sympathy call on his family—I could give them traumas, she thought—but being a philosophical type, she gave up the idea and turned on the television.

Case IV: Lillian and Frank

Lillian was an attractive married woman in her late thirties, who lived in Darien, Connecticut. Frank was a Wall Street lawyer, whose hobby was ornithology. He was married to a very pretty, but admittedly somewhat flea-brained woman named Madge, whom he liked fine until Lillian came along. Lillian engaged him in conversation at a party one night, and he was amazed to find this really attractive woman who knew the difference between a Minnesota warbler and a double-breasted nuthatch, and, what's more, cared. Besides, she was up on the finer points of Wall Street lawyering, and the deal was on when she admitted to him that she was dissatisfied with her husband, Arnold, who was just too dull and boring for words.

They arranged to meet from time to time at a small apartment in the city that Arnold kept, paid for by the company, for business entertaining. "And that's really all he does use it for," said Lillian. "The poor dope." Lillian would phone Frank at his office when she had a few free hours, she'd come in on the train, and he'd zoom up to the apartment for afternoonsies.

Lillian really took an interest in Frank's work, which, he thought, was more than Madge, who did not know a tort from third base, did. He fell into the habit of talking about his cases to Lillian, who then proceeded to solve them for him. He was amazed by her brilliance. She also bought him a book of color plates of rare birds of North America, three ties, and some undershorts. "I just can't stand those awful boxer shorts," she said. "I can't understand why Madge doesn't get you some decent ones."

Occasionally, she would cook him little lunches in the apartment, each one a gourmet delight. "It must be awful to have a wife who can't cook," she would observe on these occasions. "Poor thing. And what's more," she added, "you ought to do something about the way she dresses. Those Pucci pants she wears are entirely too tight. I mean, absolutely floozy." Frank, who up to this point had admired Madge in her Pucci pants, agreed to speak to her. Sometimes, to get a little fresh air, they would go walking in Central Park and bird-watch. Lillian could identify more birds than Frank. Other times they would go to a nearby pub that had a dart board. "I bet I can beat you at darts," Lillian said to Frank, and sure enough, she could. Other times they would go out dancing; this was not successful since Frank just could not learn the boogaloo, no matter how hard Lillian, who was an expert, tried to teach him.

One night they were having dinner at Lillian's favorite restaurant, and Frank ordered the wine. Lillian sent it back. "I should have known better than to let you order the wine," she said, studying the list. "Now what we really want is this lovely Châteauneuf-du-Pape fifty-nine." When the Châteauneuf-du-Pape '59 came, it was, as she had said, an excellent wine. "I don't know what you'd do without me, dear," said Lillian. "I don't know either," said Frank, a long-overdue steely glint coming into his eye, "but I am about to find out."

After a few weeks of phoning Frank, to no avail, Lillian gave up. Despite what she thought were mutual interests, she decided, he was really unsophisticated, a mediocre lawyer, an indifferent bird watcher, and absolutely lousy at darts. So she went to her husband, Arnold, and told him that, dull and boring as he was, she had decided to come back to him. "Good," said Arnold. "Because now you will stay home nights, and I can use the apartment again for business entertaining."

A POINT TO REMEMBER

'Tis better to have loved and lost than loved and won.

CHAPTER ELEVEN

Third Parties and the Roles They Play

The Best Friend

Every adulterous relationship seems to require at least one third party—the best friend, or confidant. This is almost a tradition. Like the man who has committed the perfect crime and blows it eventually because he has to tell *somebody* what he's done, those involved in an adulterous relationship, even when maximum security is indicated, can never really keep their big fat mouths shut, at least, not for long. The urge to tell it like it was is irresistible. (For some people, telling it is more fun than doing it, but they have special problems.) Here is where the best friend comes in. Let's face it, if Wednesday afternoons with Leon are getting to be a drag, there's nothing like your friend Genevieve's squeals of enthusiasm as you recount every last detail of what he said, and what you said, and what happened then—only doctoring it up the teeniest bit—to revive your interest no end. You may even start believing your own embellishments; this can only work to the advantage of the relationship. (It is best to pick a best friend who is patient, credulous, easily impressed, and not given to retaliating with long, tiresome analyses of *her* love life.)

Of course, it is possible to overdo this. Do not try the patience of a best friend too far. When the going gets rough, it's very comforting to be able to count on loyal Janice, who will swear that on Tuesday night you went with her to the Nelson Eddy–Jeanette MacDonald film festival and can even recite the plot of *Naughty Marietta*. So don't talk her ear off.

There are, however, some kinds of best friends that you should watch out for. Beware the best friend who wants to invite you and Alvin over to her house for dinner (there are so few places you can be seen together) or otherwise get herself involved in the situation. Men are advised to beware the friend who wants to take you and Eloise out for drinks; he'd like to meet this cookie you've talked up so much.

This kind of mixing around is no good. Take the case of George and Fred, who were best friends. Now Fred was a pleasant enough fellow, but a copycat. He always wanted what George had. When George bought a power mower, Fred bought a power mower. When George took up paddle tennis, Fred took up paddle tennis. So naturally, when George took up Sylvia, Fred wanted one, too. Well, this would have been fine if he had struck out on his own, but, oh, no, not Fred—absolutely no initiative.

George had, naturally, told Fred all about Sylvia, a lovely girl with a splendid mind, who had read every word Susan Sontag ever wrote, and when Fred asked, generous George invited him to come along for dinner at the discreet little Italian restaurant he and Sylvia had discovered.

The evening was a great success. In truth, at this

point in the relationship, George and Sylvia were beginning to run out of conversation; Sylvia couldn't grasp the nuances of direct mail advertising, and George was getting a teeny bit tired of Susan Sontag. Consequently, Fred's presence livened things up a good deal. The dinner was repeated a few times, and emboldened by his conversational success with Sylvia (his story about the account executive and the inexperienced call girl absolutely broke her up), he called Sylvia one day and asked her to have lunch. She told him she never had lunch—just cottage cheese at her desk (which should have been a warning)— so Fred, undaunted, simply arrived at her apartment at 11 P.M. one Wednesday when he knew George was speaking on Why Sex Education in Our Schools at the PTA, with a bottle of bourbon and a great big smile, and said, "Here I am, baby."

Well. That tore it. Not only did Sylvia tell Fred where he was, but the next day, she called George to tell him that just because he wasn't available, there was no need to send his lowlife friends around to entertain her, and what kind of girl did he think she was anyway, and furthermore, she was getting tired of spending time with her intellectual inferiors, whose idea of conversation was complaining about third-class mailing rates and telling dirty jokes.

As a cruel afterthought, she added some compelling reasons for sex education in our schools, using George as a horrible example, and that was the end of that.

MORAL: It is OK to confide in a best friend, but do not let him or her get into the act. A cardinal rule in creative adultery, in the words of Rudyard Kipling: "Down to

Gehenna or up to the Throne, he travels the fastest who travels alone."

The Secretary

In any extramarital relationship, it is inevitable that the woman will become involved with the man's secretary. Now, unless the girl is a complete dolt, or the woman is an absolute genius at mystification, the secretary *knows*. She pays attention to who calls him and how often, and a sudden upsurge of phone calls from a Mrs. Underhafter is going to arouse her curiosity. Therefore, it is important at the very beginning to *get his secretary on your side*.

Do not, however, attempt any buddy-buddyship with her. No first-name calling, which leads to girl-to-girl chats about how awful his wife is, even if she starts it. *Especially* if she starts it. (This does not mean she is on your side. Far from it. She is on her own side, or at least, it is safest to assume so.) Remember, secretaries are invariably attached to their bosses and apt to be jealous. This is true if he returns their affection, and even more true if he does not.

It is well early in the game to establish an identity for yourself that will make your phone calls and visits seemingly at least legitimate. Whatever your role, it should be that of some kind of benefactor or potential benefactor to the boss, so that she will snap to when you call him, but one not in any way threatening to *her*. Secretaries, remember, are where the trolley stops. They can make or break a relationship.

You might say that you are:

1. A literary agent persuading Mr. Rademacher to

write a history of the ups and downs of the electronics industry.

2. A major stockholder in the corporation whose husband just happens to be on the board of directors.

3. The wife of an extremely important client in Cincinnati.

4. His yoga instructress.

5. His mother.

Any of these roles will allay the secretary's suspicions, unless she already happens to know his mother. You can proceed from here to some small gesture of friendship. When you visit the office, inquire solicitously about her problems in keeping the files straight, getting to the office in rush hour on the subway, having psychosomatic colds. Compliment her on her desk decorations. If you sense any underlying hostility, turn it on a little. Give her some inside tips on yoga. In extreme cases, you could try soliciting her memoirs on the electronics industry or, in desperation, offer to introduce her to your husband. This only if she is really being difficult. On the other hand, if you are successful, you will be rewarded by getting your phone calls through promptly, your messages delivered, and other thoughtful gestures, like telling you where he *really* is when he says he's locked up in an all-day conference, information that you may or may not find useful at later stages of the relationship.

When the woman has a secretary, the procedure for the man is somewhat different. She, you may also assume, knows. In fact, the woman may well have told her. She can be a very useful ally. Generally, she is on your side, since she is likely to model herself on her boss and anticipate the day when she, too, will have a corner office with two windows, a secretary of her own, and a dashing married lover like you. You don't have to encourage her; she will give your messages top priority, break appointments for you, cover for her boss on those long lunch hours, assist in all manner of little ways to keep things going along smoothly. But be a little distant with her, however much you appreciate her efforts. It could be that she will decide that the corner office with two windows can wait, the secretary of her own can wait, but there you are, right now. This can lead to problems too horrible to contemplate.

The Psychiatrist

It is generally not a good idea to enter into an adulterous relationship with someone in analysis. (If it's group therapy, don't even dream of it. One Nosy Parker kibitzing from the sidelines is bad enough, but sixteen—forget it.) The psychiatrist as third party is a menace to a happy, carefree adulterous relationship. First of all, he takes sides—and *not your side*. Little he cares about the quality and progress of the relationship per se—all he's worried about is what it's doing to or for his patient.

In this situation, you are at a serious disadvantage. You are constantly aware that your friend is relating every thrilling installment of the affair to the psychiatrist. He is telling the psychiatrist all about you—and God knows what he's saying. Or, worse, what the psychiatrist is saying back. It is unnerving. You may come to feel that the psychiatrist is *using* you, like some kind of experimental animal.

You may well begin to doubt the motivation of your partner. If, for example, Gerard does something terribly sweet and totally out of character, like sending you an armload of daisies on Lincoln's Birthday or showing up on time for once, you wonder: Did he think of it all by himself, or did the shrink put him up to it?

If you must take up with some analysand, for heaven's sake, get a psychiatrist of your own so that you can fight back. But avoid the situation if possible—it's bad news.

There are, of course, exceptions. Take the case of Marvin and Ethel. Their relationship began while Marvin was in analysis. The psychiatrist thought that the affair was a good thing, since Marvin's problem was that he was overdependent on his wife, and this affair with Ethel at least got him out of the house. Then he decided that Marvin was getting as dependent on Ethel as he had been on his wife, so he blew the whistle on it. Then he decided that Marvin was now mature enough to cope with both Ethel and his wife, so it was on again.

This sequence was repeated a few times, and finally, Ethel had had it and told Marvin what he could do and that went double for that road-company Rasputin he couldn't make a move without. That was the end of it.

Well, not quite the end. A few nights later Ethel got a phone call from the psychiatrist, asking her out to dinner. "I think we should meet—I've heard so much about you," were his exact words. He turned out to be totally charming—they can be, you know—and at present, Ethel is having a perfectly divine adulterous affair with the psychiatrist, and Marvin is back being dependent on his wife, which is what he really wanted all along, so you see, these things can work out happily for all. But don't count on it.

WORDS TO LIVE BY

"If you're losing the game, change the rules."

CHAPTER TWELVE

A Word to the Working Wife

A MAJOR THESIS OF THIS BOOK IS THAT ROMANTIC LIAISONS CAN SOLVE THE PROBLEM OF THE MARRIED WOMAN who feels that homemaking is not enough. But what of the woman who doesn't have this problem, who, in fact, is happily and successfully combining career and marriage? Is she ruled out of the game? No, indeed. The working wife can, in fact, enjoy the best of all three possible worlds. The most persuasive argument we can think of for the return of married women to the labor force is the absolutely unparalleled opportunities it affords for new and exciting alliances.

Many married women have the idea that the business world is rough, tough, and competitive, and for a woman to survive in it, she must be rough, tough, and competitive, too, work around the clock, and ultimately turn herself into a neurotic, embittered shrew, a terror to the men about her and a menace to her husband and children.

This is silly. It is, to speak very plainly, a myth perpetuated by husbands to keep their wives out of the technostructure, so they can have all the fun.

The truth is that life in the private sector is infinitely more leisurely and pleasant than life at home. To begin with, there is really no work involved. All being an executive really amounts to is taking papers out of the in box, making appropriate marks on them, and putting them in

93

the out box, writing lots of memos with copies to every-body, and going to meetings. At the meetings, you are only required to keep quiet, to look thoughtful, and occasionally to agree with those of your male colleagues whom you have ascertained to be on the winning team.

Your only real responsibility is occasionally to act as house oracle on the preferences of women. (Since you are a woman, it is assumed that you know everything about the workings of the feminine mind. This is what they hire women executives for. It saves a lot of money on market research.)

Consequently, when asked if women prefer their drain cleaner in hot pink or fluorescent green containers, answer fearlessly and positively. It doesn't much matter what you say—nobody will know you goofed until later, much later, and by that time you can blame it on point of sales display or the wrong spots for the spot commercials. And if you do anything really brilliant, like suggesting that your airline set up in-flight hairdressing salons for first-class passengers (not a bad idea, as a matter of fact) or that your bank be the first with topless tellers, and if you are at all reasonable-looking, you will get your picture in *Newsweek* right away.

So you see how simple it really is. And after you have finished with the memos and the meetings, which can take several hours a week, you can spend the rest of the time having fun with the fellows. You may have heard that the business world is a sort of men's club and the woman executive is socially shunned. This may have been true in another era, when the poor men had to defend themselves in the only way they knew from a few pioneer competitive, aggressive and (usually) single females. But today's male executive is delighted by the company of a gracious, charming woman colleague, especially since she comes equipped with her own expense account. A girl who can legitimately be one of the boys, at business lunches, dinners, evening conferences, and especially out-of-town conventions is sought after indeed, and the fact that she is married, and therefore has as much to lose as they, makes it perfect.

The woman executive has unlimited opportunities for intramural romance, and extramural as well. One simple example: Suppose you have met a perfectly smashing man you're dying to know better, who just happens to be a distinguished paleontologist. Well, instead of begging your friends to invite you to dinner with him, meanwhile preparing yourself with a lot of boring conversation about Neanderthal man as you would do if you were just a housewife, hoping to attract his attention, you can decide that you need a little background on those fossilized iguana eggs your company is grinding up and putting into the face cream and hire him as a consultant at a ridiculous fee. A few late-afternoon conferences in your perfectly charming office, decorated to suit your personality in a combination of Louis XIV and neo-Bauhaus, and with its own bar and shower, and it couldn't matter less if you never heard of Neanderthal man. Or, in fact, considering the ridiculous fee, if you even look a little like him. For it is sad but true that you catch more flies with money, and lady executives have it to spend.

However, it is not the lot of every working wife to land in top management. Some must be content with more modest jobs, but this is no cause for despair. True, you cannot wheel and deal with the abandon and panache of the higher-echelon woman, but even from your lowly perch on the corporate ladder, you can stir up quite a bit of action.

Let us say you are assistant to the traffic manager of Electronic Aids and Computer Relay Systems, and you wish, so to speak, to direct some of the traffic your way. Do you accomplish this by any of the time-honored feminine come-ons, such as excessively low décolletage, provocative glances, asking him to show you how to run the Xerox machine, and so on? No, no, no. Men may talk admiringly of ladies who adopt these techniques, but it is all talk. Remember, love is to man a thing apart, and the office is where he doesn't want to get fired from. Little Miss Sexpot, the one with the oscillating miniskirt, is bad enough; Little *Mrs.* Sexpot is big trouble.

The lady executive who wishes to launch herself does her best to appear frivolous. Conversely, the nonmanagement girl must do the exact opposite. Appear dedicated to the job. Looka busy.

Your dress should be conservative, your manner serious and somewhat preoccupied. Get in there at 9 A.M., and manage traffic like crazy. Let it be known that you never go out for lunch, because that is your thinking time. When the assistant vice-president in charge of sales invites you out for drinks, say no, because you are taking an evening course in computer programming so that you can be more valuable to the organization.

Keep this routine up for at least your first few weeks on the job. Eventually, you will pique the curiosity of the men about you. Far from being categorized as big trouble, you will be regarded as a challenge. "What has a computer got that I haven't got?" is a disquieting thought indeed. Some may regard you as some kind of compulsive nut, but never mind. The more perceptive will regard you as someone worth knowing, as well as totally safe—what possible harm in being seen, say, having lunch with Miss Computer Relay Systems Expert to brainstorm a little about the Midwest sales campaign? All completely above-board and in the company interest. They will begin to envision all kinds of delightful diversions that can be carried on in the company interest. You will not have to chase the men in your office. They will chase you. If they don't, you will at least have established yourself as invaluable to the organization, as well as have learned a great deal about computers. You can't really lose.

Whom to Chase and Why

Be very cagey about whom you establish liaisons with. A safe rule is: Distance lends enchantment. Don't get mixed up with the fellow at the next desk to yours. Better another department. Also, remember the technostructure. Avoid forming attachments with men with jobs equivalent to, or lower down the scale than, yours. This creates more problems than it solves. Think upward mobile.

I.e.

Do consider: salesmen (mobile, genial, good expense accounts).

Do consider: vice-president in charge of sales (mobile, genial, et cetera. Plus more prestige).

Don't consider: the office boy (you can do better than that).

Do consider: chairman of the board (see what we mean?).

Don't consider: management consultant (conflict of interests).

Do consider: systems engineer (you learn a lot about computers).

Do consider: head of personnel (you learn a lot about a *lot* of things).

Don't consider: anyone in your car pool (limits mobility).

Don't consider: your boss (you lose a lot of jobs that way).

Do consider: his boss (catbird seat).

To sum up the advantages of being a working wife, you, too, can:

Have to work late at the office.

Go out to business lunches. ("What do you mean, attractive man? He's just some boring client I have to be nice to.")

Be entertained on expense accounts.

Have one of your own.

Ride the commuter train. (See Tips for Travelers, p. 108.)

Go to conventions in Puerto Rico. ("Of course, he has to take his secretary. How will he know what goes on if I'm not there to take notes?")

Say, when you're in over your head, "Of course, I love you, Ellsworth, and our moments together in Puerto Rico are indelibly printed on my memory. But we have to remember—I'm a married woman."

CHAPTER THIRTEEN

Some Do's and Don'ts

ON'T BECOME A FRIEND OF THE FAMILY. AVOID THE TEMPTATION TO GET EVERYBODY TOGETHER. "George, this is Fred." This is not adultery, this is sick.

DON'T indulge in true confessions. Honest is OK. But your own real life story in living color is unnecessary. Sure, you lived thirty-two years before you met Ralph, the love of your life, and you didn't hang out the whole time in the vestry of the Little Church Around the Corner. But you should generally let it seem so. Life before Ralph wasn't much. Will Ralph believe this? Yes.

DON'T flirt with sudden death by insisting that Armand take you to the restaurant frequented by your husband and all his best friends, even if it is your favorite restaurant. If food is your concern, learn to cook.

DO, if you find the magic going out of your extramarital relationship, invent a fantasy life. Pretend that you and Herbert are a pair of the great lovers of history. If you have shared a passion for poetry, you might play Elizabeth Barrett and Robert Browning. If politics, you could be Warren G. Harding and Nan Britton. Does your taste run to adventure? You can have lots of fun playing at being Mata Hari and James Bond. Or Bonnie Parker and Clyde Barrow, roaring around in your Ferrari, going "bang, you're dead" at people. There are many more to choose from. Tristan and Isolde. Lancelot and

Guinevere. Elizabeth Taylor and Richard Burton. Sonny and Chér. Let your imagination range free.

DON'T get involved with your best friend's husband. It has been proved that ten to one, friendship outlives romance. Borrow her cashmere cardigan, but not her husband. George is *hers*. If you drop him, he'll be mad at you and won't want you and Meg to be friends anymore, and if he drops you, you'll have to go on smiling through your tears of rage.

DO make complimentary remarks on all occasions. Contrary to popular belief, flattery is the sincerest form of flattery. Women, make personal remarks about his appearance (complimentary ones, you nit). Men are as vain as women. It may seem a bit much to admire a perfectly ordinary blue tie, but remember, he went into a store and picked it out himself. (Or maybe his wife did. Watch out for that.) Men, flatter—but selectively. Tell the smart ones they're pretty and the pretty ones they're smart. You can't go wrong.

DON'T call home in the presence of your partner. No matter how understanding he or she is, the sound of your voice being domestic and intimate—your *married* voice— will outrage any third party. Keep things separate.

DON'T ride your motorcycle back and forth in front of his house.

DON'T try to imitate your rival. He *has* one of those. Start with your basic image, natch (he picked you, remember) but then analyze what it is about you that seems to attract. (There must be something. If you can't think of *anything,* perhaps you need a psychiatrist more than you need a lover.) Are you clever? Do you know more about the advertising business than Doyle, Dane and Bernbach put together? Then keep up on the ad business. Don't suddenly decide that because his wife is a super soufflé maker, you suddenly have to tie on an apron and make the kitchen range your field of battle. You're the Brain Lady. Wife is the Soufflé Lady.

Or are you, on the other hand, just marvelously good-natured, feminine, perhaps just a *touch* simpleminded? And is he married to the smartest thing that ever came out of Radcliffe? Just keep pouring on the Arpège, dear, flap around in those darling pink marabou slippers, play your Jackie Gleason and Edith Piaf records to your heart's content, pour old Tired Brain his whiskey and soda, and leave the reading of *The New York Review of Books* to those who like it.

DON'T be hostile to your partner's spouse. No matter what cruel things your partner says, *you* never criticize. You do not have to elaborate to Fred about the fact that Letitia drinks too much or looks ridiculous in that curly wig—he knows that already. (Nor do you, Phil, have to make disparaging remarks to Myra about her husband's dubious earning power or the fact that he moves his lips when he reads.)

It is not enough simply not to express hostility. You ideally should not even feel it. If you have difficulty in doing this, here is a method to try. Every night before you go to bed, repeat to yourself:

Grace Festeris is a lovely woman and I like her.

Grace Festeris is a lovely woman and I like her.

Grace Festeris is a lovely woman and I like her.

DON'T complain about your own spouse. This shows lack of character. After all, it was your choice.

DON'T try to make your partner jealous. Jealousy is

the most corrosive of all emotions. Everybody (at least everybody we know) is sufficiently insecure so that he's going to be jealous anyway, so let well enough alone.

DO, on the other hand, remember to give little snarls of jealousy once in a while about the platonic friend your partner goes to the movies with occasionally. Too much jealousy is a disaster, but none at all is an insult.

DON'T play squash with her husband. If you do, don't win.

DON'T start wishing she could stay for dinner.

DO put her picture on your dresser. It will make her nervous, but she'll like it.

DON'T make funny phone calls. "Hello, this is the Acme Garage."

CHAPTER FOURTEEN

Tips for Travelers

EVERY YEAR MORE AND MORE AMERI-
CANS TRAVEL ABROAD. IT HAS BE-
COME, IN FACT, A NATIONAL HOBBY.
Now as every businessman knows, travel offers the best
possible opportunity for making new romantic alliances.
The sense of adventure, the excitement of discovering
new places, the sense of instant camaraderie so easily
established between travelers, plus the anonymity (you
hope) you enjoy in a foreign city—travel indeed has much
going for it.

The Shipboard Romance

In the movies we were raised on, the lady who travels
alone always manages to sit next to Humphrey Bogart or
Marlon Brando and looks so perfectly *happy* to be having
dinner alone on this boat that is heaving and pitching like
the devil. Suddenly her glass of wine spills in his lap, but
when he sees *who* spilled the grapes, he doesn't mind that
his new suit is ruined, and the next minute he's sitting at
her table. By the next day they're busy tracking down
German agents together.

Well, movies like this have very naturally spurred a
great interest in travel and have been the cause of a great
deal of disappointment as well. We, of course, would be
pea green in our cabin instead of up spilling glasses of

wine in *just* the right lap, and when we did get to the dining room, the guy at the next table would be a sweet, bald little fellow from Pittsburgh. By the second or third day at sea, when the fellow we wanted to meet all along finally appears on the scene, we're so monopolized by Pittsburgh that everyone else keeps away.

Keep yourself unmeshed, aboard ship, until you've had a good look around. Don't get tied up with the first fellow or girl who chats with you. You may see somebody you like lots better the very next day, but if it turns out you've already established a steady for the duration of the voyage with Early Bird, you're dead.

Instead, seek out married couples. Married couples, especially while traveling, when they are forced to talk to each other for the first time in twenty years, are usually perishing of boredom. If you're somewhat less dull than they are (which usually isn't hard), they will happily cart you wherever they go. This way you have companionship but are still in a position to negotiate, and when you do meet somebody, they won't feel abandoned or rejected or anything, but somehow instrumental. It is a prudent idea, however, if you yourself are married, to pretend to be single as far as they are concerned. Never underestimate the compulsion of the married woman to find companionship for the unattached. But although she may cheer you on if the companionship you find is married, if she knows you are, too, she is likely to get very stuffy about the whole thing.

The Airborne Adulterer, or, Fly Now, Play Later

In the prejet days, air travel allowed considerable leisure time for forming firm friendships with your fellow passengers. Not so any longer. Now it's whoosh onto a plane; drink your drink; eat your dinner; watch the movie. "We are beginning our approach to Orly [*clonk* (landing gear)], thank you for flying with us, and please do not leave your seats until the aircraft has come to a complete halt." About as much time for enriching personal contacts as if you'd been shot there by a missile.

However, all is not lost. To meet anyone on a plane these days requires speed, daring and expertise, but it can be done.

Look at it this way. No matter how short the flight time, your seatmate is your captive audience for the duration of it. And you can accomplish a lot in five and a half hours. During that time you make polite conversation, borrow each other's magazines, have cocktails, enjoy a gourmet dinner, catch a movie (there are those who hold that the in-flight movie is the greatest stimulus to mobile adultery since the drive-in), and finally sleep, scrunched up against each other's shoulders. (By this time, you may well have removed the armrest.) The equivalent of two weeks' courtship (in some cases a two-year engagement) under ordinary circumstances. However, first you have to assure yourself of the proper seatmate. This is best accomplished if you observe the Mercer-Peterson first law of aerodynamics: *Always travel first*.

For women, it is always worthwhile to travel first class, even if you have to pay the difference out of your lunch money. Only men travel first class—prosperous and important men, usually without their wives. Tourist class is full of honeymoon couples, nuns, hubby-mommies with children that yell a lot and get sick, and twenty-two-year-old sailors clutching pictures of their girl friend in Terre Haute.

First class, on the other hand, is full of solid and mature types who will be surprised and pleased to see a lady traveling first. In this convivial atmosphere, where the booze flows free, and there are no old ladies grabbing for the sick sack, you will immediately be labeled as very rich or an important business executive, neither of which labels, contrary to common belief, ever did a girl any real harm.

First class, except at certain peak travel seasons, is generally half-empty. This leads to great mobility, getting up and changing your seat, and so forth. Also, it makes it easier to pick your seatmate. Here is how it is done. Before flight time, hang around the first-class lounge, VIP Room, or whatever they call it. Size everybody up. Give everybody a chance to size you up. Then, girls, get right on the plane and establish yourselves in a window seat. Men, linger. When you get on the plane, never mind your assigned seat. Sit next to the lady of your choice. If somebody else is sitting there, and doesn't look too formidable, try to trade seats with him ("I have to sit near the front of the plane because of my asthma") or persuade him that he is in the wrong seat. A thoughtful tip to the steward will assure you official backing in this endeavor. Simple? Experienced travelers have been doing it for years.

If you have bad luck with your seat partner, circulate. If it is one of those planes that has a lounge in the back, sit there. If you see someone you fancy sitting next to an empty seat, jump up on it and lean over to catch a last glimpse of Fire Island. Or take pictures out the window. Take his or her picture, too. At cocktail time, get up and walk around, drink in hand, and make conversation with various groups. Get some action going.

Advice to men: Forget stewardesses, despite those commercials in which certain airlines push their stewardesses as if they were running the white slave trade or something. Stewardesses have a built-in suspicion of passengers. If you want to meet an airline stewardess, go to one of those swinging singles pickup joints on New York's East Side, disguised as an account executive from Papert, Koenig and Lois.

Things to carry on airplanes: booze. Especially girls. Always carry a pint in your purse. You never know when the plane is going to be stalled on the ground for two hours in a dry state or out at the end of the runway or someplace else where they can't serve. Your very own supply is a great icebreaker and will earn you the lifelong gratitude of drinkers who forgot to bring theirs.

A camera. This enables you not only to look out of somebody's window, but to take pictures out of it. And of them, too. In fact, a camera is vital equipment, not for taking pictures of the Acropolis by moonlight or the canals of Amsterdam, but for taking pictures of people. Then you bring the contacts around to their hotel later and—

Things people will want to borrow:

Nail file.

Scissors, needle and thread.

The Story of O.

The Miami *Daily News*.

There are many opening gambits for making friends on planes. Borrowing matches, newspapers, etc. are fine for shy types. General conversation is rather expected. One experienced traveler we know always says to the man next to her as they taxi up the runway, "I'm just terrified during takeoff. Would you hold my hand?" Works wonders.

Trains

Cross-country train travel is not what it was in Mary McCarthy's day. Forget trains. Except the commuter train. A smashingly turned-out lady commuter is bound to attract admiring glances in this all-male atmosphere. But remember the ground rules. A commuter train is essentially a men's club. Do not take anybody's seat, kibitz at card games, or offer bright suggestions on the *Times* crossword puzzle. Find your own seat, get your own crossword puzzle, beam happily at everyone, and who knows what may happen?

Where to Go—U.S.A.

One of the best places in the whole world to meet people is the Great American West. Throughout the West it is considered OK, in fact, customary, for women to sit at bars and converse in a friendly fashion with fellows they just met. This is in sharp contrast with Connecticut, a state that so mistrusts the motives of women that it won't let them sit at bars *at all*. This accounts for the fact that there are practically no bars in Connecticut. Fellows feel silly sitting there alone. Forget Connecticut. Also forget New York. There the bars either take a dim view of women or are so full of swinging singles swinging away that you have a better chance of developing a civilized relationship on the Lexington Avenue express platform at rush hour. Consider particularly the possibilities of California. In California it is considered absolutely OK, if not mandatory, to make a close personal friend of everybody in sight. If you spot a likely type walking along the street, it is perfectly permissible to walk up to that person and say, "Hello. I love you." If you can't manage this sort of thing, they have places where, for somewhat less than the price of a weekend at the Fontainebleau, you can combine resort life with group therapy sessions that teach you how. (You have to admit, Grossinger's hasn't thought of *that*.)

Where to Go—Europe

In European cities, the friendly camaraderie of the Western saloon does not obtain. The woman traveling alone is cold-shouldered in the bars and jolly public meeting places of European cities.

For this reason, it takes a little more ingenuity for women to meet people in Europe. Here are some ideas.

In London: Wander around Soho with a large map of the city. The map enables you to stand in one place and peer over top to get a good look at somebody before you ask him or her how to get to Sotheby's.

In Paris: Head straight for the Faubourg St.-Honoré. Go into an expensive handbag shop, and in an animated fashion, go about selecting an expensive handbag for your sister in Sioux Falls. Have a long, earnest discussion with the saleswoman about the relative merits of several handbags, and before you actually have to buy one, you will be approached by at least one bashful American man who wants you to help him pick out a handbag for his wife

Voilà. A charming companion. And just possibly a handbag.

In Moscow: Easiest place in the world. Just sit in the lobby or dining room of an Intourist hotel and look like an American. You will be approached by a traveling West German businessman who wants to tell you how great the Americans are and how rotten the Russians are, traveling Scandinavians want to tell you how rotten the Americans are and how great the Russians are, traveling Englishmen who want to tell you how rotten the Russians are and how great the Red Chinese are, traveling Americans who want to tell you that their room is bugged, they keep hearing this clicking noise, and long-haired Russian teen-agers who want to mooch a joint of pot. Take your pick.

In Rome: Sit in the Sistine Chapel with a small mirror to help you admire the painting on the ceiling. Ask all the interesting-looking people you see if they know that Michelangelo originally painted everyone in this scene stark naked. When someone says yes, continue the conversation.

In other cities (we haven't actually been to very many) if you want to go places where men are welcome and women are generally not, get a movie camera, preferably the big kind with tripod, and lug it around with you wherever you go. Say you are making an underground movie. Otherwise, carry an ordinary camera—not so much for taking pictures but for help in changing film. All men can change camera film, just as they all can change tires. It's an instinct. Also, many a fellow too shy to say, "Hello," finds it much easier to say, "Hello, is that a Zeiss Ikon?"

Great Pickup Joints Around the World

London: Poets' Corner, Westminster Abbey.
Venice: Top of the Campanile.
Rome: Via Veneto. Sistine Chapel.
Amsterdam: Diamond Exchange.
Paris: Eiffel Tower.
Moscow: Lenin's Tomb.
Capri: Axel Munthe's house.
New York: Central Park Zoo.

Places to Stay Away from

Hippie communes.
The Île du Levant.
Topless barbershops.
Le Drugstore.
The Tower of London.
The Leaning Tower of Pisa.
Fort Lauderdale.

CHAPTER FIFTEEN

Organized Adultery

Don't mourn for me, boys—organize.

—JOE HILL

E HAVE RECEIVED MANY QUERIES ABOUT THE ADVANTAGES AND DIS- ADVANTAGES OF KEY CLUBS, WIFE- swapping groups, and the like. This is distressing. Why do Americans have to make a club out of everything? We are, to be blunt, not enthusiastic about wife-swapping clubs, although we realize that they are very popular in some parts of the country. We feel that the regimentation of the club defeats the real purpose of creative adultery, which is, of course, self-development and self-realization and the achievement of inner harmony, and that these organizations, although they start off with the best of in- tentions, often degenerate into mere gang bangs. We be- lieve that the best and most constructive interpersonal relations are conducted on an individual rather than a group basis.

However, if you must join a club, look carefully into the club you join. Some adultery clubs that we have heard of are run by unscrupulous individuals who collect dues (key money is what it is called) from members, sup- posedly to be used for such purposes as building a social center, establishing scholarships in the club name, legal aid for members who need it, and so forth, but are actually used to pay handsome salaries to the board of directors. Be sure your club is financially aboveboard. Be sure, also, that it is not discriminatory in any way. Inquire if membership makes you eligible for charter flights. (One ingenious group we know of has pooled its funds to buy an overage DC-7, so that members, for fares less than half of those charged by commercial airlines, can carry on in Hong Kong, Cairo, Seattle, Washington, or wherever fancy dictates, thus combining horizontal enrichment with the broadening influence of travel.)

Another deplorable form of organized adultery is the computer date bureau. We have had many inquiries about the desirability of finding partners this way. All we can say to those who have this kind of naïve faith in computers is: Haven't you had enough trouble with your department store bills?

CHAPTER SIXTEEN

How Should the Injured
Wife Behave?

EORGE IS HAVING AN *AFFAIR*. WELL,
THERE IT IS. YOU TRIED TO THINK
FOR A LONG TIME THAT HE REALLY
was working late at the office, but it has finally come
through to you that there's more to it than that. What to
do? First, keep calm. Consider the situation realistically.
Realize, first of all, that you're holding most of the cards.
From now on, it's how you play them that counts.

Your relationship, yours and George's, has now em-
barked on a new era. It can be your finest hour and prepare you both for those lovely Golden Years together at
Sunny Acres Retirement Estates.

You were lovers once, but that was a while ago. Then
you had the long, secure nesting or hubby-mommy stage,
acquired children, furniture, a five-bedroom house with
four, count 'em, four bathrooms, a nice portfolio of stock,
and twenty pounds of hip fat.

And now George, good, steady George, to whom
you've given your whole life, your (once-removed) virginity, and every waking thought, is doing this terrible
thing. George, who is definitely developing a bald spot on
the back of his head. George, who jogs around the reservoir every morning it doesn't rain; George, who cracks
his knuckles, George, who won't, won't eat eggs any way

but scrambled, George, in other words, who is *yours,* is doing this terrible thing.

Look at it this way. You are now embarking on a third wonderful adventure in the history of your togetherness. You can laugh at it together, later, at Sunny Acres. Provided you proceed sensibly, don't yell or make scenes, and get to Sunny Acres.

You have a delicate role to play. In the old days, when you were lovers, you had *that* to hold you fast. Then, in the hubby-mommy era, you were a person of some importance. Who else knew how the formula was made? But now you're being held up for scrutiny against a thirty-six-year-old lady engineer—one broken marriage, no children, no hip fat, and a new Jaguar she bought for herself. *Quel paragon.* OK, so you can't snorkel, know nothing about mechanical engineering, no longer have either Young Passion or the Mother role to fall back on. What *do* you have? (Well, not much, frankly.) But what you do have is number one position. The ability to make his life living hell—take his car, children, most of his money, and enlist a lot of sympathy along the way. But don't do it. You'll wind up with a car you can't drive very well, children going off to join the Peace Corps, and a lot of friends who will eventually get tired of your complaints.

What you have to be now is the Good Old Girl Who's Known Him Forever. Now don't be obnoxious about it and keep going on about those two-tone shoes he wore when he first went to Dartmouth, Ho Ho Ho, or how you used to beat him at tennis—be nice about it. You, only *you,* know how he likes his eggs, that he prefers soggy toast, adores shad roe, Western movies, and Benny Goodman, so now you become the great dispenser of shad roe, kindliness, creature comforts, gentle humor, and all that. Faintly maternal. Essentially he's a comfort-loving fellow, hates fights, scenes, etc. Just wants to have this one teeny-weeny little affair, is all. And doesn't he deserve it, after all, after a lifetime of riding the 8:12 to the Rostock Insurance Company? If you think about it, you know he does. Makes him feel very Foreign Legion.

The role of nag is not a pretty one and won't get you anywhere anyway. It may scare him, but it won't scare him out of what he's doing; it will merely scare him into being more devious. Nor will outrage or tears. Though, (and this is important) a good fit of outrage can keep him within civilized bounds—home for dinner on time and all that. But keep outrage fits short. They can be construed merely as a demonstration of affection and concern. (He doesn't want to think that you don't give a damn.) This would be an impossible blow to his ego. But just don't go on and on and be boring about it. Being Mrs. Sad Face will just make him all the fonder of Mechanical Engineering.

You might try a few oblique ploys if you know who she is. (What a nice girl! Why does she wear those funny shoes?) But there's not too much in this really, apart from the satisfaction.

Keep everything smiles across the miles for the first six months at least, no matter how hard it gets. After that it's likely that the first teensy-weensy little twinge of boredom with her will set in, and then you can shake the branches a bit.

But really, if you're half as smart as you think you are, you will realize that what you have been handed is a license to steal. Use it. Send all the kids to Camp Minnetonka for the summer and take off with Aunt Alice for Angkor Wat. This way, you won't be sitting home being Sad and Blue; he will. He will be delighted, at first, poor nit, with a whole free summer—not realizing, of course, that it was the cloak and dagger that made the lady engineer so riveting. By August he'll be terribly dragged with bringing his own shirts to the laundry and tearing around Rhode Island in that damned Jaguar. When you get home, thinner (lose some weight, for God's sake!), tanner, with some funny little expressions you picked up from an adorable guide called Pnomptang, and the glorious glamorous aura of world traveler replacing that faint dishwater scent you used to have, you may find that the whole problem has solved itself.

CHAPTER SEVENTEEN

How Should the Injured Husband Behave?

OUISE IS HAVING AN *AFFAIR*. LOUISE? GOOD, OLD, EASYGOING LOUISE, WHO TURNS UP FAITHFULLY WITH THE station wagon every night to meet the 6:02 in her old beat-up polo coat, who spends her days uncomplainingly taking kids to the dentist, painting the ceilings, freezing quantities of *boeuf bourguignon* so that it doesn't matter how many people you bring home for dinner. Never complaining, always agreeable, whose biggest thrill in the last six months was the time you got two tickets for *Hello, Dolly!* and the two of you had an evening on the town. And now this. First of all, it's a little hard to believe. Now if it had been that redheaded South American divorcée that Chet Schroeder married—but Louise. She's not much to look at, and, let's face it, a little dull. It can't be true.

However, it is. And what are you going to do about it?

Now this is supposed to be, according to popular theory, the most difficult of all situations for men to accept. It isn't. There are many ways in which, if you are clever, you can save your marriage, as well as save face.

The traditional male response to discovering a wife's infidelity, is to threaten to strangle the SOB with his bare hands, if not, indeed, to do so. In fact, this is the only thing a proper Italian husband can justifiably do, and the proper Italian wife who did not inspire this response would feel unloved and unappreciated. Don't, however, strangle anybody with your bare hands, or anything else. It's too messy, and besides, it's against the law. You might, however, react with a suitable amount of rage and violence. Not directed at the man—this is, after all, a family matter—but at your wife. You don't have to really rough her up, just rage around, growl ferociously, throw things, and make dire threats. This may scare the wits out of her or merely prompt her to say, "Oh, come off it, Alvin," depending on her personal style, but either way it will impress her that you really love and cherish her. Every woman wants to feel that her husband is a hairy-chested brute at heart, and knocking her about a bit might be just the thing to fan the sparks of your dying relationship into a roaring furnace.

But perhaps you don't want any roaring furnace; you just want to keep things the way they are. In that case, take another tack. Ignore the whole thing. Act as if nothing is happening. When you hear her creeping in the back door with her shoes off at 12.30 A.M., shout down and tell her to be sure to put the latch on the screen door, because the hinge is loose, and when the wind blows, it bangs. Refrain from asking nastily who that overaged hippie is that she has over afternoons to play pot and sympathy with, even though the neighbors, who have charted his comings and goings carefully are asking *you*. Continue to be gallant and attentive. Or if you weren't before (and let's face it, you weren't, before), start. Make brilliant conversation at the dinner table. Exude charm.

Show her what she's got to lose. (She may have thought nothing, you know.) In any case, it's by far the best way of sitting out this very probably temporary situation.

Meanwhile, take heart. Look on the bright side. You will find your wife, while illuminated by the pleasures of her infidelities, a most charming companion. Full of good humor and cheer. Instead of making her daily rounds feeling that life is dull, stale, flat, and unprofitable, she will be all smiles and inclined to fix you nice little surprises at dinner. In fact, her newly aroused libido may present you with some little surprises you never anticipated. The unfaithful wife is not nearly so bad as tradition demands the injured male think—the frivolous female has it all over Little Dolly Goodwife, who mopes around and eats candy bars all day. In fact, you may, once you get used to the idea, enjoy the side effects of your wife's new hobby. And don't forget, the situation presents you with ample justification for doing likewise. So what are you waiting for, you silly man?

CHAPTER EIGHTEEN

The End of the Affair

ANY ADULTEROUS RELATIONSHIPS FLOURISH HAPPILY FOR A LIFETIME. HOWEVER, EVEN WITH TRUE LOVE, membership in the same therapy group, a common interest in urbanology, and strict adherence to all the rules in this book, the magic can go out of your extramarital relationship. We don't like to bring this up, but it is true.

There are little signs that tell you when it's time to call it quits.

When you (the man) break a date because you really have to work late at the office. When you (the woman) do so because you've just had your hair done and don't want it messed up. When either cancels out because there's something you're dying to watch on television. When your wife or husband suddenly looks more attractive than your light of love. Or, more to the point, when someone else does.

Now, if life were as perfect as we would like it to be, you should be able to just walk out and say *adios* when the magic fades. This works in those rare instances when both parties decide to detrain at the same time. But this almost never happens. One person usually has to take the initiative.

"I don't love you anymore, so forget it, Charlie," will not do. It is sad but true that when one person wants out, the other often starts to cling all the more tightly, to complain vociferously, and generally to make a mess. This suffering is not so much from love's loss, much as you may want to think so, but from severe damage to the ego—which can be more painful.

If not handled properly, this situation can be very sticky, if not downright dangerous. The rejected partner sometimes gets very angry and threatens to tell all, to kill you or (the more sporting type) to kill himself. It can get scary.

The kind way, as well as the prudent way, is to make the rejected one think it was his idea. Or, if it wasn't, that it should have been.

Some Approaches to Try

> "I don't love you anymore because you don't love me anymore. But you don't know it yet."

> "I'm beginning to bore you, I know, and I think we should call it quits before I bore you too much, because then you would leave me, and I couldn't stand that."

> "Nothing in life could be more perfect than our relationship, and I think we should stop it right now while it's at the utter peak of perfection."

> "I used to love you a little, but now I love you too much for your own good, so I'm not going to see you anymore, and besides it's interfering with my Russian language class."

> "I need to go away and just *think* about you for a while."

> "I love you so much that I'm gaining weight. When I get to one hundred forty, good-bye."

> "I love you so much that I'm losing weight. When I get to one hundred forty, good-bye."

These approaches should work. (At the least, the rejected partner may be so dazed by the logic involved that he will decide you have lost a few marbles and run for it.) If he doesn't, more direct evasive action may be required.

SUCH AS:

Saying that Harvey has found out and is threatening to kill me.

Saying that Harvey has found out and is threatening to kill you.

Saying that you're planning to hike the entire length of the Appalachian Trail next summer.

Doing it.

Becoming a Carmelite nun.

Moving to Los Angeles.

Now this may all be much too straightforward—not to say inconvenient—for you. But there is one other approach. We have been saving it for last, because although difficult to carry off, it is almost foolproof. *Become unlovable.*

Most people are too vain to carry this off successfully. Also, it sometimes happens that as you start to make yourself unlovable and the other person starts to pull away from you, you decide that you love him (her) madly after all and want him (her) back. But that is the risk you take. Becoming unlovable has almost never been known to fail.

How to Become Unlovable

Don't bathe.

Don't shave.

Wear your hair in rollers in the daytime.

Wear your hair in rollers in the daytime covered by a little pink wrinkled chiffon scarf that says "Santa Catalina Island."

Wear a sweat shirt that says "I'm a swinger."

Play Perry Como records all the time.

Talk too loud in restaurants about how you *feel* about things.

Take up paddle tennis, and don't talk about anything else.

Take up wildlife conversation, and don't talk about anything else.

Buy a transistor television and carry it around all the time.

Say, "Right!" all the time.

Wear paste-on sideburns.

Ride your motorcycle past his house.

Make funny phone calls. "Hello. This is the Acme Garage."

Get tattooed.

How to Get Left with Dignity

Now it sometimes happens that the one who gets rejected isn't Walter or Florence, as the case may be. It is *you*. This is one of the most difficult situations you will encounter as you pursue your career of creative adultery. Few people deal with it intelligently. This is a shame, because it can be, if handled properly and considered in its true perspective, an ultimately rewarding experience. It requires you to call on resources you didn't know you had (maybe you don't?), to develop new spiritual muscle—in short, to become a better person.

At least, that is what happens in the long run. In the short run, before all that spiritual muscle develops, it is advisable to have some suitable, dignified replies on tap for the moment of truth.

When he starts, timorously, to tell you that he's going to be faithful to his wife from now on, so it's *sayonara* to you baby, giggle. When he asks for an explanation, say, "That's what I *thought* you were going to say."

When he says, "Bye," say, "Right!"

Say you learned a lot.

Say you didn't learn much.

Say, "Oh, poo."

Shake his hand and say you're glad he's finally seeing it your way.

Don't try to make him jealous by alluding to other fellows in your life. Instead, say thoughtfully that after this experience you may just forget the whole thing for a while.

Tell everyone you had to leave him because he refused to take a firm stand on basic issues.

Ask him if he's making any headway with his sex problem. Don't explain.

When It's All Over

So now it is over. You have successfully disentangled yourself from (or have been successfully disentangled by) Walter or Florence (*that's* a relief), and you are at peace with the world. You may be sadder and wiser or happier and stupider, but no matter. You have gained by the experience. No matter how disastrous the denouement (and it shouldn't have been too bad—God knows, we *tried*), you have grown. You have beautiful memories to look back on. Your home is intact. Your children are ecstatic, now that you no longer have to work nights. Emily (or Ronald) has forgiven you (if, indeed, she ever knew). You have forgiven yourself. (Wasn't hard, was it?) What happens next?

WELL, YOU:

Bathe.
Shave.
Throw away your rollers.
Burn your swinger sweat shirt.
Remove your tattoo.
Simonize your motorcycle.
And start afresh. (See Chapter 3, page 30, How to Begin.)